GET BY IN

SPANISH

D1471557

A QUICK BEGINNER'S COURSE FOR HOLIDAYMAKERS AND BUSINESS PEOPLE

ISABEL DEL RÍO-SUKAN

BBC BOOKS

Published by BBC Books
a division of BBC Enterprises Ltd
Woodlands
80 Wood Lane
London W12 0TT

First published 1992
© Isabel del Río Sukan 1992

ISBN 0 563 36135 2

Designed by Peter Bridgewater
Map and Illustrations by Lorraine Harrison
Cover Illustration by Tony Masero

Set in Great Britain by
Central Southern Typesetters, Eastbourne
Printed and bound in Great Britain by Clays Ltd, St Ives plc

Cover printed by Clays Ltd, St Ives plc

Exclusive U.S. Distributor of the Get By in Series Packs

Ambrose Video Publishing, Inc.
1290 Avenue of the Americas
Suite 2245
New York,
N.Y. 10104

CONTENTS

MAP SHOWING
SPANISH-SPEAKING
COUNTRIES

1 USA
2 MÉXICO
3 GUATEMALA
4 EL SALVADOR
5 NICARAGUA
6 COSTA RICA
7 HONDURAS
8 PANAMÁ
9 CUBA
10 REPÚBLICA DOMINICANA
11 PUERTO RICO
12 VENEZUELA
13 COLOMBIA
14 ECUADOR
15 PERÚ
16 BOLIVIA
17 CHILE
18 ARGENTINA
19 URUGUAY
20 PARAGUAY
21 GUINEA ECUATORIAL
22 ESPAÑA
23 FILIPINAS

1. 19,500,000	9. 9,880,000	17. 11,682,000
2. 73,641,000	10. 5,962,000	18. 29,627,000
3. 6,526,000	11. 3,350,000	19. 2,968,000
4. 5,232,000	12. 14,940,000	20. 3,117,000
5. 3,058,000	13. 27,500,000	21. 304,000
6. 2,379,000	14. 8,200,000	22. 39,310,000
7. 4,092,000	15. 18,707,000	23. 2,900,000
8. 2,089,000	16. 6,082,000	

INTRODUCTION

The new BBC *Get By in Spanish* course aims at providing basic, practical knowledge to all those who want to learn Spanish, whatever their language abilities.

The course includes a book and two cassettes with five units, each dealing with specific areas of conversation: Hello, Shopping, Out and About, Getting to your Destination and Living in Spain. Each unit includes the following:

- Dialogues related to the subject of each unit;
- Language explanations, to dispel any doubts you may have;
- Exercises, for you to practise your knowledge of Spanish;
- A list of key words and phrases used in the conversations, as well as additional items of vocabulary.

The *Get By* audio cassettes provide you with the basic language you will need to get by and 'survive' in Spanish. They include real life conversations with Spaniards to give you a 'feel' of Spain, and also enable you to get the flow and speed of the real language. There are also a number of repetition and conversation exercises to allow you to practise your Spanish. The two bilingual presenters will guide you through the course, providing practical help and hints.

The *Get By* book includes the text of the recorded conversations and explains in detail the language which is being used. It also includes exercises to enable you to assess your knowledge of Spanish as you proceed through the course. Each unit in the book has a Worth Knowing section too, with brief but factual background information on Spain, its people and their customs. You will also find a Reference Section at the end of the book, together with a Key to the Exercises.

TO MAKE THE MOST OF THE COURSE

As this is a self-teaching course, motivation varies from one person to the next. Nevertheless try to:

● Get used to the sounds of the language by listening to the cassettes after reading the book;

● In the pronunciation practice sequences, repeat out loud what you are asked to say. There are a number of repetition exercises in the cassettes, with pauses for you to give the correct answer;

● Go through the Explanation sections, and check for any new words in the Key Words and Phrases section or in the Word Lists;

● Either write out the exercises in the book or say them out loud. They will help you to get the flow of the language.

Keep in mind that:

● Learning is best achieved through practice and enjoyment;

● Learning should be done at one's own pace, but ideally you should try to practise on a regular basis, a little at a time.

● The course aims to teach, entertain and inform.

We wish you good luck with your Spanish . . . *¡Mucha suerte!*

1 HELLO

KEY WORDS AND PHRASES

¡Hola!	Hello
¿Qué tal?	How are you? How are things?
¿Cómo está?	How are you? (formal)
¿Cómo estás?	How are you? (informal)
bien	well
muy bien	very well
gracias	thank you
muchas gracias	thank you very much
buenos días	good morning
buenas noches	good evening, good night
buenas tardes	good afternoon
adiós	goodbye
hasta luego	see you later
soy . . .	I'm . . .
me llamo . . .	I'm called . . .
mi nombre es . . .	my name's . . .
me llaman . . .	they call me . . .
¿Cómo se llama usted?	What's your name? (formal)
¿Cómo te llamas?	What's your name? (informal)
¿Qué va a tomar?	What are you going to have?
un café	a coffee
por favor	please
una cerveza	a beer

sí	yes
no	no
el vino blanco/tinto	white/red wine
el agua mineral (f.)	mineral water
¿Qué tienen para beber?	What do you have to drink?
¿Tienen . . .?	Do you have . . .?

CONVERSATIONS

The following conversations are included on the cassette. Listen to them carefully. The important words or phrases are listed above, but look up any other words you don't understand in the Word List following the conversations.

HELLO! HOW ARE YOU?

SUSANA   Hola.
FELISA   Hola.
CARLOS   Hola, ¿qué tal?

FELISA   ¿Cómo está?
CARLOS   Bien, ¿y usted?
FELISA   Muy bien, gracias.
CARLOS   Hola, Susana. ¿Cómo estás?
SUSANA   Muy bien, ¿y tú?
CARLOS   Bien, bien.

GREETINGS AND GOODBYES

SEÑOR   Buenos días, señora.
SEÑORA   Buenos días.

SEÑORA   Buenas noches.
SEÑORA   Hola, buenas noches. ¿Qué tal?

SEÑOR   Adiós, buenas tardes.
SEÑOR   Adiós, hasta luego.

WHAT'S YOUR NAME?

I'm . . .

PABLO	Hola, ¿qué tal? Soy Pablo, Pablo García González. ¿Y tú?
ISABEL	Hola, soy Isabel.
ISABEL	Buenos días. ¿Cómo se llama usted?
Mª JOSE	Yo me llamo María José Velasco Ulazia.
ISABEL	Buenos días. ¿Cómo se llama usted?
PEPE	Buenos días. Mi nombre es Pepe Luna.
ISABEL	Hola, buenas noches. ¿Cómo te llamas?
LOLA	Me llamo Dolores Arránz Martín. Me llaman Lola.

GETTING A COFFEE

ISABEL	¡Oiga, camarero!
CAMARERO	Buenos días. ¿Qué va a tomar?
ISABEL	Un café, por favor.
CAMARERO	¿Solo o con leche?
ISABEL	Con leche.
CAMARERO	¿Leche fría o caliente?
ISABEL	Caliente, por favor. Gracias.

AT THE BAR

ISABEL	¿Qué tienen para beber?
CAMARERO	Cerveza, naranja, limón, vino blanco, vino tinto, agua mineral . . .
ANA	¿Tienen tapas?
CAMARERO	Sí. Champiñones, calamares, tortilla española, jamón, chorizo . . .
ISABEL	Sólo cerveza.
ANA	Cerveza también y . . . champiñones.
CAMARERO	Dos cervezas y champiñones. Muy bien.

WORD LIST

beber	to drink
un café con leche	a white coffee
un café solo	a black coffee
los calamares	squid
caliente	hot
el camarero/la camarera	the waiter/waitress
con	with
los champiñones	mushrooms
el chorizo	Spanish salami-type sausage
frío/a	cold
el jamón	ham
la leche	milk
un limón	a lemon drink or the fruit
una naranja	an orange drink or the fruit
o	or
¡Oiga!	Excuse me! Hey!
sólo	only, just
también	as well, also
la tortilla española	Spanish omelette
tú **usted** }	you
y	and
yo	I

EXPLANATIONS

1 GREETINGS AND GOODBYES

Hola means 'hello'; *adiós* means 'goodbye'. But you can also use the following to greet or say goodbye to someone: *Buenos días* (in the morning), *Buenas tardes* (in the afternoon and early evening), *Buenas noches* (in the evening and at night), *hasta luego* or *hasta mañana* ('see you tomorrow'). You can use them together too:

EXAMPLES:
Hola, buenos días
Adiós, buenas noches, hasta mañana

2 HOW ARE YOU?

Tú and *usted* both mean 'you'. *Tú* (informal) is used for family, friends and among young people; *usted* (formal) is used for people you don't know very well. To ask 'How are you?' say:
¿Cómo está usted? or *¿Cómo está?* (formal)
¿Cómo estás tú? or *¿Cómo estás?* (informal)
Note that you don't necessarily have to say *usted* or *tú*.
And to reply:
Muy bien, gracias. ¿Y usted? (formal) or *¿Y tú?* (informal)

In written Spanish (e.g. signs in public buildings) you may see *Vd.* or *Ud.* – the shortened form of *usted*, and *Vds.* or *Uds.* for *ustedes* (the plural).

¿Qué tal? is a very useful expression which you can use to ask 'How are you?', 'How are things?' or when you're introduced to someone. It can also be used to ask what something's like:
EXAMPLES:
¿Qué tal? (formal and informal) How are you?
¿Qué tal estás? (informal)
¿Qué tal está? (formal)
¿Qué tal el café? How's the coffee?
¿Qué tal todo? How's everything?

3 WHAT'S YOUR NAME?

Ways of saying what your name is: *Soy . . .* , or *Mi nombres es . . .* or *Me llamo . . . .* You only need to use one version.

Many Spaniards use the shortened version of their name.
EXAMPLE:
Mi nombre es Francisco. My name is Francisco. *Me llaman Paco.* They call me Paco.

How you ask someone their name again depends on how formal you want to be:
¿Cómo se llama? or *¿Cómo se llama usted?* (formal)
¿Cómo te llamas? (informal) What are you called?

4 BEING POLITE AND ATTRACTING SOMEONE'S ATTENTION

In Spanish, unlike English, it is still considered polite to make a request without using *por favor* or *gracias* when given something. *De nada* is a common response to being thanked and means 'not at all' or 'you're welcome'.

When you want to attract someone's attention (e.g. a waiter) you can just say:
¡Oiga! or *¡Oiga, por favor!* or *¡Oiga, perdone!* (a more polite version).

5 WHAT ARE YOU GOING TO HAVE?

A waiter in a bar or cafe will ask you:
¿Qué va a tomar? or *¿Qué van a tomar?* (when referring to several people)
You can reply by just saying what you want:
Un café solo or *un vino blanco*
Or you can say:
Quiero una cerveza. I want a beer.
Quiero un café. I want a coffee.
If you're having a white coffee, you might be asked:
¿Leche fría o caliente? Hot or cold milk?
(NOTE: SPANISH COFFEE IS NOT SERVED WITH CREAM.)

6 ASKING WHAT THERE IS TO DRINK AND EAT

To ask what there is to drink you say:
¿Qué tienen para beber?
There's usually quite a choice:
un té a cup of tea

un vaso de agua a glass of water
una copa de coñac a glass of brandy
un vino rosado rosé wine
una copita de jerez a small glass of sherry
un zumo de naranja an orange juice
So when you hear *¡Vamos a tomar una copa!*, it means 'Let's go and have a drink!'

Most bars in Spain serve *tapas*. To find out what's on offer ask:
¿Tienen tapas? Do you have any tapas?
There might be:
aceitunas (f.) olives
jamón (m.) ham
calamares (m.) squid (ringed and fried)
ensaladilla (f.) potato salad
pescado frito (m.) fried fish
gambas (f.) prawns
chorizo (m.) Spanish salami with Paprika
The range is literally endless!

7 MASCULINE AND FEMININE

In Spanish, like in other languages, words are either masculine or feminine. *El café* is masculine, *la cerveza* is feminine, and so on. This means that words that go together have to 'match'.
EXAMPLES:
La (f.) *cerveza* (f.) *está buena* (f.) The beer is good
El (m.) *vino* (m.) *está bueno* (m.) The wine is good

It's a question of practice knowing which word is feminine and which masculine, although when you're talking about people it's obviously easy to know.
EXAMPLES:
La (f.) *señora* (f.) The woman/lady
El (m.) *señor* (m.) The man

8 PLURALS

In Spanish, you have to add an -*s* for the plural:
café, cafés coffee, coffees
When the word ends with a consonant you add *es:*
champiñón, champiñones mushroom, mushrooms
ciudad, ciudades city, cities

9 THE, A AND SOME

There are several ways of saying 'the' in Spanish, either masculine or feminine, and either singular or plural:

	SINGULAR	PLURAL
Masculine	*el*	*los*
Feminine	*la*	*las*

EXAMPLES:
el café, los cafés the coffee, the coffees
la cerveza, las cervezas the beer, the beers

The words for 'a' and 'some' also change according to whether the word referred to is masculine or feminine:

	SINGULAR	PLURAL
Masculine	*un*	*unos*
Feminine	*una*	*unas*

EXAMPLES:
un café, unos cafés a coffee, some coffees
una cerveza, unas cervezas a beer, some beers

10 ADJECTIVES

Adjectives must also 'match' the name. This is how *bueno* ('good') changes:

	SINGULAR	PLURAL
Masculine	*bueno*	*buenos*
Feminine	*buena*	*buenas*

EXAMPLES:
El café está bueno The coffee is good
Los calamares están buenos The squid are good
Las cervezas están buenas The beers are good
(NOTE THAT *ESTÁ* ('IS') BECOMES *ESTÁN* ('ARE') IN THE PLURAL.)

Adjectives which end in *-e* are the same for masculine and feminine.
EXAMPLES:
el café caliente hot coffee
la leche caliente hot milk
So are adjectives which end with a consonant:
un coche azul a blue car
una blusa azul a blue blouse
BUT NOT ADJECTIVES OF NATIONALITY:
un vino español a Spanish wine
una señora española a Spanish lady
You must still add an *-s* or *-es* in the plural.
EXAMPLE:
español, españoles

In Spanish the adjective generally follows the noun:
vino tinto as opposed to 'red wine'.
There are exceptions, however:
Buenos días, Buenas tardes, etc.
(SEE REFERENCE SECTION FOR MORE ADJECTIVES AND COLOURS.)

EXERCISES

GREETINGS AND GOODBYES

1   It's 9.00 a.m. How would you greet your friend Tomás? Also ask him how he is.
2   How would you say 'Goodbye'? It is 10.00 p.m.
3   Ask Mrs González how she is.
4   A friend asks you how you are. What would you reply?

AT THE CAFETERIA

5   Call the waiter.
6   Ask for a white coffee.
7   Ask for a beer.
8   Ask for white wine and some olives.

MIX AND MATCH

9	Buenos	fría	12	Vino	días
10	Buenas	solo	13	Café	tardes
11	Agua	tinto			

FILL IN THE GAPS

14 Hola, buenos _____ . ¿Cómo _____ usted?
    Muy bien, _____ . ¿Y _____ ?
15 ¿Qué va a _____ ?
    _____ café.
    ¿Solo _____ con leche?
    Con leche, _____ _____ .
16 Soy Pepe. ¿ _____ tú?
    _____ Carlos.
17 ¿ _____ estás?
    Bien, _____ . ¿ _____ tú?
18 ¿ _____ tal?
    _____ bien. ¿Y_____ ? (formal)

IN A BAR

Ask what drinks they have:
19 _____

Cerveza, vino y agua mineral.
Now ask if they have *tapas*:
20 _____
Tortilla, aceitunas y jamón.
Now make your choice – beer and ham:
21 _____

TRANSLATE INTO SPANISH

22 How's the beer?
23 I want a coffee.
24 Red wine, please.
25 No, thank you.
26 The beer is good.
27 The wine is cold.

WORTH KNOWING

BARS AND CAFES – *BARES Y CAFETERIAS*

There are no licensing restrictions in Spain, so bars and cafes usually remain open until late at night. Drinks are generally cheaper in Spain than in other European countries. The Spanish custom is to have a drink along with appetisers or *tapas*.

TITLES

Señor (*Sr.* for short) referring to a man
Señora (*Sra.*) referring to a married or older woman
Señorita (*Srta.*) referring to a young woman

NAMES AND SURNAMES

Spaniards generally use two surnames: the first one is the father's surname, and the second one the mother's.
EXAMPLE: Dolores Arránz Martín

In Spain, women do not change their surname when they marry, although they can be called by their husband's surname when being addressed as Mrs or *Sra.*
EXAMPLE: Carmen Rigau Monedero, wife of Antonio García Salvador, can also be called Sra. García, or Sra. de García. Their children, by the way, will have two surnames: García Rigau.

You will also sometimes hear *Don*, for a man, or *Doña* for a woman. It's used for elderly people, or as a sign of respect.
EXAMPLE: Don Juan (or D. Juan), Doña Julia (or D$^{\underline{a}}$ Julia).

2 SHOPPING

KEY WORDS AND PHRASES

¿Hay?	Is/are there any?
¿Cuánto valen?	How much do they cost?
un cuarto de kilo	a quarter of a kilo
¿Qué tipo tiene?	What sort have you got?
este es de Cataluña	this is from Catalonia
¿A cuánto es el kilo/litro?	How much is it per kilo/litre?
medio kilo	half a kilo
¿Cuánto es?	How much is it?
aquí tiene	here you are
¿Qué desea?	{ May I help you? / What would you like?
¿Cuánto queso quiere?	How much cheese do you want?
¿Algo más?	Anything else?
nada más	nothing else
¿Cuánto es en total?	How much does it all come to?
quiero . . .	I want . . .
un sello	a stamp
¿Tiene . . . ?	Do you have . . . ?
¿Tiene algo para la tos?	Have you got anything for a cough?
son	(they) are
¿Cuál prefiere?	Which one do you prefer?
¿Vende . . . ?	Do you sell . . . ?
¿Me puede dar . . . ?	Could you give me . . . ?

¿Qué precio tiene?	How much is it?
¿En qué puedo servirle?	May I help you?
¿Qué número?	What shoe size (do you take)?
¿Le gustan éstos?	Do you like these?
estos me gustan mucho	I like these a lot
¡Qué caro!	How expensive!
más barato	cheaper
cambiar	to change
una libra (esterlina)	a pound (sterling)
de compras	shopping

CONVERSATIONS

GETTING SOME RED APPLES

ISABEL	¿Hay manzanas rojas?
TENDERA	Sí, señora.
ISABEL	¿Cuánto valen?
TENDERA	Cien pesetas el kilo
ISABEL	Dos kilos, por favor.

HOW MUCH IS THE HAM?

ISABEL	Un cuarto de kilo de jamón serrano. ¿Qué tipo tiene?
TENDERA	Este es de Cataluña.
ISABEL	¿A cuánto es el kilo?
TENDERA	A dos mil pesetas.

GETTING SOME TOMATOES

ISABEL	Medio kilo de tomates, por favor.
TENDERO	Muy bien.
ISABEL	¿Cuánto es?
TENDERO	Cuarenta y cinco pesetas.
ISABEL	Aquí tiene. Muchas gracias.

AND A FEW GROCERIES

TENDERA	¿Qué desea?
ISABEL	Dos litros de aceite de oliva, un kilo de arroz y un poco de queso manchego . . .
TENDERA	¿Cuánto queso quiere?
ISABEL	Unos . . . doscientos gramos.
TENDERA	Muy bien. ¿Algo más?
ISABEL	No, nada más, gracias. ¿Cuánto es en total?
TENDERA	Pues . . . novecientas ochenta pesetas.

AT THE POST OFFICE

MARGARITA	Quiero veinte sellos para Europa.
EMPLEADO	¿Cuántos sellos?
MARGARITA	Veinte. ¿Cuánto es en total?
EMPLEADO	Cuarenta y cinco pesetas cada sello . . . novecientas pesetas.

AT THE CHEMIST'S

ISABEL	¿Tiene algo para la tos?
FARMACEUTICO	Estas pastillas son muy buenas.
ISABEL	¿Cuánto valen?
FARMACEUTICO	El paquete pequeño ciento cincuenta y cinco, y el paquete grande doscientas setenta. ¿Cuál prefiere?
ISABEL	El pequeño, por favor. Aquí tiene, ciento cincuenta y cinco.

GETTING A FOREIGN NEWSPAPER

EXTRANJERO	¿Vende periódicos extranjeros?
VENDEDOR	Sí, claro.
EXTRANJERO	¿Me puede dar el Times?
VENDEDOR	Sí, sí.
EXTRANJERO	¿Qué precio tiene?
VENDEDOR	Doscientas veinte pesetas.
EXTRANJERO	Muchas gracias.

GETTING A PAIR OF SHOES

EMPLEADA	¿En qué puedo servirle?
ISABEL	Quiero unos zapatos negros.
EMPLEADA	¿Qué número?
ISABEL	El treinta y siete.
EMPLEADA	A ver . . . ¿le gustan éstos?
ISABEL	Sí. Estos me gustan mucho. ¿Qué precio tienen?
EMPLEADA	Siete mil setecientas cincuenta.
ISABEL	¡Qué caro! ¿Tiene algo más barato?
EMPLEADA	No, no hay nada más barato. Lo siento.
ISABEL	Bueno, lo pensaré. Adiós, buenos días.

CHANGING MONEY

ISABEL	Buenos días. Quiero cambiar unas libras.
EMPLEADA	¿Cuántas libras?
ISABEL	Quinientas.
EMPLEADA	A ver, la libra esterlina . . . a ciento setenta y cuatro, coma cero seis pesetas. Quinientas libras son en total . . . ochenta y siete mil, treinta pesetas.

WORD LIST

a ver	let's see
el aceite de oliva	olive oil
el arroz	rice
cada	each
el color	colour
el empleado/la empleada	employee, clerk
Europa (f.)	Europe
el extranjero/la extranjera	foreigner
extranjero/a	foreign
el farmacéutico/la farmacéutica	chemist
la farmacia	chemist's

grande	large, big
hoy	today
el jamón serrano	cured ham
un kilo	a kilo
un litro	a litre
lo pensaré	I'll think about it
lo siento	I'm sorry
una manzana	an apple
más	more, plus
el modelo	design, style (of clothing), model
negro/a	black
el paquete	box, packet
las pastillas	tablets, pastilles
el pequeño/la pequeña	the small one
pequeño/a	small
el periódico	newspaper
un poco de . . .	a little . . .
el queso (manchego)	cheese (from the *La Mancha* area)
rojo/a	red
sí, claro	yes, of course
el tendero/la tendera	shopkeeper
la tienda	shop
el tomate	tomato
el vendedor/la vendedora	vendor, salesman/woman
los zapatos	shoes

EXPLANATIONS

HAY/¿HAY?

Hay is a very useful word which literally means 'There is . . ./
'Is there . . . ?'/'There are . . .'/'Are there . . . ?'
It can be used to enquire if something is available.

EXAMPLES:

¿Hay huevos? Are there are any eggs?/Do you have any eggs?

Sí, hay Yes, there are
No, no hay huevos No, there aren't any eggs

Instead of *¿Hay . . . ?* you can ask the shopkeeper:

¿Vende . . .? (plur. *¿Venden . . . ?*) Do you sell . . . ?

¿Tiene . . .? (plur. *¿Tienen . . . ?*) Do you have . . . ?

ASKING THE PRICE

If you want to know the price of something, use:
¿Cuánto valen?
¿Cuánto cuestan? } How much do they cost?
¿Cuánto vale?
¿Cuánto cuesta? } How much does it cost?
¿Qué precio tiene? How much is it?
¿Qué precio tienen? How much are they?

Or if you want to know the specific price per kilo or per litre:
¿A cuánto es el kilo?
¿A cuánto es el litro?

When you want to know how much you have to pay, use:
¿Cuánto es? or *¿Cuánto es en total?*
REPLIES:
Son cien pesetas 100 pesetas
Son dos mil quinientas 2500 pesetas
(SEE THE LIST OF NUMBERS IN THE REFERENCE SECTION.)

WHAT WOULD YOU LIKE?

The shopkeeper will ask you:
¿Qué desea? or *¿En qué puedo servirle?*
You can either just say what you want to buy or use *quiero* meaning 'I want'.
EXAMPLES:
Un kilo de manzanas or *Quiero un kilo de manzanas*
Un litro de vino or *Quiero un litro de vino*

Keep in mind that in Spanish you don't necessarily have to say 'I', 'you', 'he', etc., because it's clear from the verb ending which person you're referring to.

EXAMPLES:

Yo quiero un kilo = *Quiero un kilo* I want a kilo
¿Vende usted jamón? = *¿Vende jamón?* Do you sell ham?

HOW MUCH DO YOU WANT?

EXAMPLES:

¿Cuánto queso quiere?
¿Cuánto jamón quiere?

This changes if the items you want are plural:

¿Cuántos limones quiere?
¿Cuántos huevos quiere?

Or feminine:

¿Cuántas manzanas quiere?

REPLIES:

medio kilo half a kilo
un cuarto de kilo a quarter of a kilo
un poco a little, a bit
unos doscientos gramos about 200 grammes

ANYTHING ELSE?

You'll be asked:

¿Algo más?

REPLIES:

Sí, también quiero . . . Yes, I also want . . .
No, nada más, gracias No, nothing else thanks

NEGATIVES

In Spanish, 'no' and 'not' are both *no:*

No quiero café I do not want any coffee
No hay vino blanco There is no white wine Or:
No, gracias No, thank you

AT THE POST OFFICE

Buying stamps (see also Worth Knowing at the end of this unit):

Quiero un sello para el Reino Unido I want a stamp for the UK
Quiero un sello para Europa I want a stamp for Europe
Quiero un sello para España I want a stamp for Spain

Or when you want to send something:

Quiero enviar una postal I want to send a postcard
Quiero enviar una carta urgente I want to send an express letter
Quiero enviar una carta certificada I want to send a registered letter
Quiero enviar un telegrama I want to send a telegram
Quiero enviar un paquete I want to send a parcel

AT THE CHEMIST'S

¿Tiene algo para . . . Can you give me something for . . .

la tos? a cough?
el dolor de cabeza? a headache?
el dolor de estómago? a stomach ache?
el dolor de oídos? an earache?
la indigestión? indigestion?
la insolación? sun stroke?
las quemaduras de sol? sun burn?

REPLIES:
una pastilla a tablet, pastille
unos supositorios some suppositories
un jarabe cough mixture
unas gotas some drops
una crema a cream

EXAMPLES:
Estas pastillas son muy buenas. These tablets are very good.
Este jarabe es muy bueno. This cough mixture is very good.

THIS, THESE, THAT, THOSE

'This' and 'these' also have to match the word they refer to:

	SINGULAR	PLURAL
MASCULINE	*este*	*estos*
FEMININE	*esta*	*estas*

EXAMPLES:
este jamón this ham
estas manzanas these apples

When you don't name something or when you point at something without naming it, use *esto*:

EXAMPLE:
¿Cuánto vale esto? How much is this?

For 'this one' and 'these ones' (i.e. when they don't precede a noun) use *éste, éstos* or *ésta, éstas*:
No quiero éste I don't want this one
Quiero éstos I want these ones
In written Spanish an accent is added, but the pronunciation is the same.

'That' and 'those' match the masculine or feminine word too:

	SINGULAR	PLURAL
MASCULINE	*ese*	*esos*
FEMININE	*esa*	*esas*

EXAMPLES:
esa botella that bottle
esos huevos those eggs

When you don't name something or when you point at something without naming it, use *eso:*
EXAMPLE:
¿Cuánto vale eso? How much is that?
For 'that one' and 'those ones' use *ése, ésos* or *ésa, ésas*:
Quiero ésos I want those ones

No quiero ése I don't want that one
These also have an accent in the written form, but the
pronunciation remains the same.

I LIKE

Me gusta ('I like') literally means 'it pleases me'. Remember
that *gusta* is for the singular and *gustan* for the plural.
EXAMPLES:
Me gusta el vino I like the wine
Me gustan estos zapatos I like these shoes

There are two forms to use for 'do you like?':
INFORMAL:
¿Te gusta el queso? Do you like (the) cheese?
¿Te gustan los tomates? Do you like (the) tomatoes?
FORMAL:
¿Le gusta España? Do you like Spain?
¿Le gustan las tapas? Do you like 'tapas'?

REPLIES:
Sí, me gusta Yes, I like it
No, no me gustan No, I don't like them
You can also reply:
Me gusta muchísimo I like it very much
Me gusta mucho I like it a lot
Me gusta bastante I like it quite a lot
Me gusta un poco I like it a little

But when you definitely don't like something:
No me gusta nada I don't like it at all
No me gustan nada I don't like them at all

You can also say:
Me encanta/encantan I love it/them
Prefiero otro tipo/color/modelo I prefer another sort/colour/design

EXTRA SHOPPING ITEMS

LOS COMESTIBLES	GROCERIES
un kilo de azúcar	a kilo of sugar
una barra de pan	a loaf of bread
una botella de vino	a bottle of wine
un paquete de galletas	a packet of biscuits
la mantequilla	butter
la mermelada	jam
la mermelada de naranja	marmalade
un pastel	a cake
una docena de huevos	a dozen eggs
media docena de huevos	half a dozen eggs
LA FRUTA	FRUIT
las fresas	strawberries
los melocotones	peaches
un melón	a melon
las peras	pears
los plátanos	bananas
las uvas	grapes
LAS VERDURAS	VEGETABLES
el ajo	garlic
las cebollas	onions
los espárragos	asparagus
las espinacas	spinach
los guisantes	peas
una lechuga	a lettuce
las patatas	potatoes
los pimientos	peppers
las zanahorias	carrots
LAS PRENDAS DE VESTIR	CLOTHING
un abrigo	a suit
una blusa	a blouse
una camisa	a shirt

una chaqueta	a jacket
un par de botas	a pair of boots
un par de calcetines	a pair of socks
un par de medias	a pair of stockings, tights
un par de pantalones	a pair of trousers
un par de zapatos	a pair of shoes
un traje	a suit
un vestido	a dress
DON'T FORGET:	
el número	shoe size
la talla	clothes size
OTROS ARTÍCULOS	OTHER ITEMS
un bañador	a swimsuit
unas gafas de sol	sunglasses
una guía	a guide book
un plano de la ciudad	a street map

EXERCISES

AT THE GROCER'S

Here's your shopping list:
  half a kilo of grapes
  quarter of a kilo of Serrano ham
  two litres of red wine
  four kilos of tomatoes

You're in the grocer's:
Buenos días, ¿qué desea?
Ask for all the items on your list:
1 _____
¿Algo más?
Tell him you don't want anything else and ask how much it is:
2 _____
The grocer tells you the amount:
Son mil cuatrocientas veintisiete.

You give the shopkeeper the money and say 'Here you are':

3 _____

MIX AND MATCH

In Spain, you would buy *jamón* at a *jamonería,* so where would you buy . . .

4	la leche (milk)	**a**	una frutería
5	la carne (meat)	**b**	una pescadería
6	el arroz (rice)	**c**	una carnicería
7	las verduras (vegetables)	**d**	una pollería
8	el pescado (fish)	**e**	una verdulería
9	la fruta (fruit)	**f**	una lechería
10	el pollo (chicken)	**g**	una panadería
11	el pan (bread)	**h**	una tienda de comestibles

AT THE CHEMIST'S

Ask the chemist to give you something for an earache:

12 _____

Estas gotas son muy buenas.

Now ask him to give you something for sun burn:

13 _____

Esta crema es estupenda (wonderful).

Now ask him how much everything is:

14 _____

Son ochocientas treinta pesetas.

Now say: 'Here you are. Thank you very much. Goodbye.'

15 _____

AT THE SHOE SHOP

You want to buy a pair of brown shoes, size 42:

16 _____

The shopkeeper says: *'Tengo este modelo. Son doce mil quinientas pesetas'.* Tell the shopkeeper you find these shoes very expensive, and ask him if he has anything cheaper:

17 _____

He brings you another pair of shoes: *'Tengo este otro modelo. Son diez mil pesetas. ¿Le gusta?'*
Tell him that you don't like them at all, and ask if he has another design (*modelo*):

18 _____

AT THE POST OFFICE

Ask for five stamps for Europe:

19 _____

Now say that you want to send a postcard:

20 _____

MIX AND MATCH

21 Una blusa	negros
22 Unas camisas	rojo
23 Unos zapatos	blancas
24 Un abrigo	amarilla

(SEE LIST OF COLOURS IN THE REFERENCE SECTION.)

FILL IN THE BLANKS

25 Buying a suit:

SEÑORA	Buenos días. _____ un _____ .
EMPLEADA	¿De _____ talla?
SEÑORA	La cuarenta.
EMPLEADA	¿Le gusta _____ ?
SEÑORA	Sí, _____ me _____ mucho.
	¿ _____ precio _____ ?
EMPLEADA	Veintitrés mil ochocientas _____ .
SEÑORA	¡ _____ caro! ¿Tiene algo más _____ ?
EMPLEADA	No, no hay _____ más barato. Lo _____ .

WORTH KNOWING

THE MARKET – *LA PLAZA*

In Spain, you can buy food in individual shops, but also in *la plaza,* a large covered market which houses a number of stalls. Many towns have *un mercado* (street market) on certain days of the week. Both the *plaza* and the *mercado* are ideal places to practise the language you have learnt in this unit.

There are also many supermarkets (*supermercados*) for all your shopping, and in larger cities even huge hypermarkets (*hiper-mercados*), where you can buy anything from food to furniture.

THE WINE SHOP – *LA BODEGA*

You can buy wine by the litre, a *granel,* and you can even bring along your own container and have it filled with your favourite drink! *Bodegas* usually serve drinks as well.

SPANISH WINE – *EL VINO ESPAÑOL*

Spain is a leading wine-producing country. As a result of a most favourable climate, there are 57 wine-producing districts, so wine-tasting in Spain can be quite an experience. These are the more popular wines:

● *Jerez* or sherry, the most famous Spanish wine, which some call 'bottled sun'. It originates from the town of Jerez de la Frontera, near Cadiz, southern Spain, and there are many varieties.

● *Rioja,* the classic wine, from northern Spain.

● *Cava,* the Spanish version of champagne, from the Penedés district in Catalonia.

● Spanish whisky – although scotch is very popular with Spaniards, Spain boasts its own brand of whisky, with distilleries in Segovia, just north of Madrid.

You can visit most Spanish vineyards by prior appointment, and there are also a number of wine festivals held all over Spain throughout the year.

THE CHEMIST'S – *LA FARMACIA*

In Spain chemists are qualified pharmacists, who can actually give you advice on general ailments. The *farmacia* has a green cross above the entrance. Outside normal working hours and on bank holidays, there's only one on-duty chemist open in each area (*la farmacia de guardia*). You will find a list of 'who's open when' displayed in the window of every local chemist's.

THE POST OFFICE – *CORREOS*

At the *Oficina de Correos,* or just *Correos,* you can post letters or send telegrams (telegram service available only in some post offices).

THE TOBACCONIST – *EL ESTANCO*

At the *estanco* you can buy stamps and postcards as well as cigarettes: *tabaco* or *cigarrillos*. Virginia-style tobacco is called *el tabaco rubio* and black tobacco, *el tabaco negro*. Black tobacco brands are usually produced nationally, and are therefore much cheaper. You will recognize the *estanco* from the 'T' displayed outside (which stands for *Tabacalera,* the state-owned tobacco company).

BANKS – *LOS BANCOS*

Opening times: Monday to Friday 0900 – 1400 hrs and Saturdays 0900 – 1300 hrs. Banks are closed on Saturdays from June to September. You will also find branches of European and international banks in the main cities.

The Spanish currency is *la peseta. Pts.* is short for *pesetas.* Coins: 1, 5, 10, 25, 50, 100, 200, 500 pesetas.
Notes: 1000, 2000, 5000, 10000 pesetas.

3 OUT AND ABOUT

KEY WORDS AND PHRASES

¿Dónde . . . ?	Where . . . ?
¿Dónde está . . . ?	Where is . . . ?
está aquí mismo	it's just here
la primera a la derecha	the first on the right
la segunda a la izquierda	the second on the left
a unos tres minutos a pie	about three minutes on foot
todo recto por la calle Princesa	straight ahead along Princess Street
¿Cómo dice?	Pardon. What did you say?
en el número 265	at number 265
¿Hay un banco por aquí?	Is there a bank around here?
allí mismo	just there
enfrente de	opposite
¿Está lejos el Museo del Prado?	Is the Prado museum far?
¿Cómo puedo ir?	How can I get there?
¿Sabe qué autobús?	Do you know which bus?
la parada (del autobús)	bus-stop
la parada (del Metro)	the tube station
no sé	I don't know
no comprendo	I don't understand
soy extranjero/a	I'm a foreigner
¿Qué hora es?	What's the time?
¿Tiene hora?	Have you got the time?

¿Me puede decir . . . ?	Can you tell me . . . ?
¿A qué hora abren/cierran?	What time do you open/close?
¿Se puede . . . ?	Can one . . . ? May I . . . ?
¿Individual o doble?	Single or double?
Para mí solamente	Just for me
¿Con baño o sin baño?	With or without a bathroom?
¿Me permite ver su pasaporte?	May I see your passport?
¿Cuánto es por noche?	How much a night is it?

CONVERSATIONS

WHERE IS . . . ?

ISABEL   Oiga, perdone . . . ¿dónde está la calle de Toledo?

TRANSEUNTE   Pues, está aquí mismo. La primera a la derecha, y luego la segunda a la izquierda.

EXCUSE ME . . . .

SUSANA   Oiga, ¿la Plaza de España?

TRANSEUNTE   Está a unos tres minutos a pie. Todo recto por la calle Princesa y está al final.

LOOKING FOR A CHEMIST'S

PABLO   Perdone, ¿dónde[1] hay una farmacia?

TRANSEUNTE   ¿Cómo dice?

PABLO   Una farmacia.

TRANSEUNTE   Ah, muy cerca, en el número 265 de esta calle, a unos cien metros aproximadamente.

LOOKING FOR A BANK

JOSE   Oiga, ¿hay un banco por aquí?

TRANSEUNTE   Sí, muy cerca. Mire, allí mismo. Enfrente del estanco.

IS IT FAR?

MONTSE	Oiga, ¿está lejos el Museo del Prado?
TRANSEUNTE	Lejos no; lejísimos. Está en el centro.
MONTSE	¿Cómo puedo ir?
TRANSEUNTE	En taxi . . . o en autobús.
MONTSE	¿Sabe qué autobús, por favor?
TRANSEUNTE	No sé . . . el veintisiete o el diez, creo.
MONTSE	¿Y dónde está la parada?
TRANSEUNTE	Mire, allí enfrente.

SAYING YOU DON'T UNDERSTAND

ISABEL	Oiga, por favor. ¿Dónde hay una cabina de teléfonos?
EXTRANJERO	No comprendo.
ISABEL	¿No comprende español?
EXTRANJERO	Muy poco . . . soy[4] extranjero.
ISABEL	Ah, es extranjero. ¿Y está aquí de vacaciones?
EXTRANJERO	Sí, sí. Soy extranjero y estoy aquí de vacaciones.

WHAT TIME IS IT?

ISABEL	¿Qué hora es, por favor?
FELISA	La una y diez.
PABLO	¿Tiene hora?
PALOMA	Sí, las once y veinticinco.
PABLO	Gracias.
PALOMA	De nada.
CARLOS	¿Me puede decir la hora, por favor?
FELISA	Son las cuatro menos cuarto.

AT WHAT TIME . . .?

MARGARITA	¿A qué hora abren el museo?
EMPLEADO	A las nueve y media de la mañana.
MARGARITA	¿Y a qué hora cierran?
EMPLEADO	A las siete de la tarde.

CAN YOU . . .?

PALOMA	Oiga, ¿se puede aparcar aquí?
POLICIA	No, aquí no. Está prohibido.
RAQUEL	¿Se puede comer en el restaurante?
CAMARERO	No, señora. Ahora está cerrado.
CARLOS	¿Se puede fumar?
AZAFATA	No, lo siento. Esta es la zona de no fumadores.

CHECKING IN AT A HOTEL

ISABEL	Buenos días, quiero una habitación.
RECEPCIONISTA	¿Qué tipo de habitación? ¿Individual o doble?
ISABEL	Individual. Para mí solamente.
RECEPCIONISTA	¿Con baño o sin baño?
ISABEL	Con baño.
RECEPCIONISTA	¿Para cuántas noches?
ISABEL	Seis noches.
RECEPCIONISTA	Seis noches, muy bien. ¿Me permite ver su pasaporte?
ISABEL	Sí, aquí tiene. ¿Cuánto es por noche?
RECEPCIONISTA	Diez mil quinientas pesetas, más los impuestos. ¿Tiene equipaje?
ISABEL	Sí, estas dos maletas.
RECEPCIONISTA	Estupendo. Pues, aquí tiene la llave. Habitación trescientos veintidós.

WORD LIST

el aeropuerto	airport
ahora	no
aparcar	to park
aproximadamente	approximately
la azafata	air hostess
el banco	bank
la cabina de teléfonos	telephone box
la calle	street
la catedral	cathedral
el centro	the centre
cerca	near
cerrado/a	closed
comer	to eat
creo	I think
de la mañana	a.m.
de la tarde	p.m.
de nada	not at all, you're welcome
de vacaciones	on holiday
en	in, at
en autobús	by bus
en metro	by tube
en taxi	by taxi
el equipaje	luggage
el español	Spanish (language)
la estación	station
el estanco	tobacconist's
estupendo/a	wonderful, great, marvellous
al final	at the end
fumar	to smoke
la habitación	room
la hora	hour, time
un hospital	hospital
el hotel	hotel

los impuestos	taxes, VAT
lejísimos	extremely far away
luego	then, later
la llave	key
la maleta	suitcase
¡Mire!	Look!
Perdone	Excuse me. Sorry
el policía	policeman
la policía	police
prohibido/a	forbidden, not allowed
el/la recepcionista	receptionist
el restaurante	restaurant
los servicios	toilets
el taxi	taxi
la tienda	shop
el/la transeúnte	passer-by
el tren	train
la zona de no fumadores	non-smoking area

EXPLANATIONS

1 ASKING DIRECTIONS

When you want to know where something is use:
¿Dónde está . . . ?
EXAMPLES:
¿Dónde está la Plaza Mayor?
¿Dónde está el Hotel Goya?
Or in plural:
¿Dónde están los servicios?

To ask 'Where is there a . . . ?' use:
¿Dónde hay una farmacia?
¿Dónde hay un estanco?
¿Dónde hay un hospital?

Asking 'Is there a . . . ?'
¿Hay una cabina de teléfonos por aquí?
¿Hay una frutería en esta calle?

REPLIES:

Está . . .	It's . . .
aquí mismo	just here
allí mismo	just there
a la derecha	on the right
a la izquierda	on the left
a unos cien metros	about 100 metres away
en la plaza	in the square
en el número 5 de esta calle	at number 5 in this street
Carretas esquina Sol	on the corner of Carretas Street and Sol Square

Or you can say:
lejos far
muy lejos very far
lejísimos extremely far away
cerca near
muy cerca very near
cerquísima extremely near

2 HOW TO GET THERE

When you want to know how to get somewhere ask:
¿Cómo puedo ir a . . . ?
EXAMPLES:
¿Cómo puedo ir al aeropuerto?
¿Cómo puedo ir a la estación?

You might get there:
en autobús by bus
en metro by tube
en taxi by taxi
a pie/andando on foot

3 SAYING YOU DON'T
KNOW OR DON'T UNDERSTAND

If you're asked for information and you can't help, say:
No sé
If you didn't understand something and want it repeated, say:
¿Cómo? or *¿Perdone?* or *¿Cómo dice?*

You can say that you don't understand:
No comprendo
You can also say that you don't understand Spanish:
No comprendo español
Or that you don't speak Spanish:
Lo siento. No hablo español

You could also explain that you're a foreigner:
Soy extranjero/a

4 TO BE – *SER* AND *ESTAR*

In Spanish, there are two ways of saying 'to be': *ser* and *estar*.
The verb *ser* refers to *what* you are:
¿Es usted extranjero? Are you a foreigner?
Sí, soy inglés Yes, I'm English
The verb *estar* refers to *where* you are:
¿Dónde estás? Where are you?
Estoy en España de vacaciones I'm in Spain on holiday
El Sr González está en viaje de negocios Sr González is on a
business trip

EXAMPLE: ⁻
Soy extranjero y estoy aquí de vacaciones I'm a foreigner and I'm
here on holiday

Estar can also be used to say *how* you are:
¿Cómo estás? How are you?
Estoy bien, gracias I'm fine, thanks

Or *how* things are:
La cerveza está buena The beer's good
El vino está frío The wine's cold

5 WHAT TIME IS IT?

In Spanish, you can use any of these:
¿Qué hora es?
¿Tiene hora?
¿Me puede decir la hora?
You can, of course, add *por favor* in order to make your request more polite:
¿Qué hora es, por favor?

Telling the time in Spanish you have to say:
Son las . . .
EXAMPLE:
Son las siete It's seven o'clock

There's an exception, though: for one o'clock, use *Es . . .* :
Es la una It's one o'clock

To say 'past', add *y*:
Son las siete y cinco It's five past seven
Son las siete y diez It's ten past seven
Son las siete y cuarto It's quarter past seven
Son las siete y veinte It's twenty past seven
Son las siete y veinticinco It's twenty-five past seven
Son las siete y media It's half past seven

To say 'to', add *menos*:
Es la una menos veinticinco It's twenty-five to one
Es la una menos veinte It's twenty to one
Es la una menos cuarto It's quarter to one
Es la una menos diez It's ten to one
Es la una menos cinco It's five to one

When you want to specify a.m. or p.m., you have to add the following after the time:

de la mañana in the morning or a.m.

de la tarde in the afternoon or p.m.

de la noche at night, after 9 p.m.

EXAMPLES:

Las nueve de la mañana 9.00 a.m.

Las cuatro y media de la tarde 4.30 p.m.

A las once menos cuarto de la noche At 10.45 p.m.

Son casi las cinco de la mañana It's nearly 5.00 a.m.

Al mediodía At midday

A medianoche At midnight

Las diez   *Las doce y cuarto*   *Las tres y media*   *Las ocho menos cuarto*

6 OPENING AND CLOSING TIMES

Abierto Open / *Cerrado* Closed

To ask at what time a place opens:

¿A qué hora abren?

EXAMPLES:

¿A qué hora abren el museo? (the museum)

¿A qué hora abren las tiendas? (the shops)

¿A qué hora abren el bar? (the bar)

REPLY:

A las nueve de la mañana

To ask at what time a place closes:

¿A qué hora cierran?

REPLY:

A la una de la tarde

You might want to ask other things:

EXAMPLES:

¿A qué hora . . .   What time . . .

  sirven el desayuno?   do you serve breakfast?

  sirven la comida?   do you serve lunch?

  empieza la película?   does the film start?

7 CAN, CAN'T

Things you can do:

Se puede visitar el museo del Prado You/one can visit the Prado museum

Se puede nadar You can swim

Se puede tomar el sol You can sunbathe

Things you can't do:

No se puede comer en el hotel You/one can't eat at the hotel

No se puede ir en autobús You can't go by bus

No se puede visitar la catedral, está cerrada You can't visit the cathedral, it's closed

How to ask:

¿Se puede fumar? Can one/Can you/May I smoke?

¿Se puede aparcar aquí? May I park here?

¿Se puede ir en metro? May I go by tube?

The expression *¿Se puede?* on its own means 'May I?' You can use *¿Se puede?* to get past people in a crowded place, just before entering a room, to take an extra chair in a restaurant or bar, etc.

When asking for information you can make your request more polite by starting the question with:

¿Me puede decir . . . ? Can you tell me . . . ?

EXAMPLES:

¿Me puede decir la hora?

¿Me puede decir dónde hay una farmacia?

¿Me puede decir dónde están los servicios

8 AT THE HOTEL

If you want to book a room:
Quiero reservar una habitación para tres noches. I want to book a room for three nights.
Quiero reservar una habitación para una semana. I want to book a room for a week.

If you're asking about available rooms, you have to say:
¿Tienen una habitación, por favor?

You'll be asked what type of room you want:
¿Qué tipo de habitación quiere?
REPLIES:
individual/doble single/double
con baño/ducha with bathroom/shower
con dos camas/cama de matrimonio with twin beds/double bed
con vistas al mar/a la montaña with views of the sea/mountains
para dos noches for two nights
interior overlooking an inner courtyard
exterior overlooking the street

EXERCISES

IN THE STREET

Ask a passer-by where the museum is:
1 _____

Now ask him where there's a chemist's:
2 _____

Now ask him if there is a bus-stop nearby:
3 _____

I'M A FOREIGNER

Somebody stops you in the street and asks you something.
Say that you're sorry and that you don't speak Spanish:
4 _____

And add that you're a foreigner:

5 _____

GETTING TO THE PLAZA DE ESPAÑA

Ask how you can get to the Plaza de España:

6 _____

Está muy lejos. Se puede ir en autobús.

Ask the passer-by if he knows what bus:

7 _____

El M-3, creo.

Now thank him/her and say goodbye:

8 _____

FILL IN THE GAPS

Finding your way

ISABEL	Oiga, _____ . ¿Dónde _____. una farmacia?
SEÑOR	En _____ calle Mayor.
ISABEL	¿Está _____ ?
SEÑOR	No, está _____ cerca. A unos dos _____ a pie.
ISABEL	Muchas _____ .
SEÑOR	_____ nada.

TELL THE TIME

10 12.15
11 9.30
12 3.10 p.m.
13 It's nearly 1.00
14 6.50

15 1.25
16 It's nearly 2.45
17 At 11.00 a.m.
18 At 12.45 p.m.
19 At 10.55 p.m.

ASKING DIRECTIONS

See the map opposite and then answer these questions:

20 ¿Hay una farmacia cerca de la Plaza Mayor?

21 ¿En qué calle está el Museo de Cervantes?
22 ¿Dónde está la parada del autobús?
23 ¿En qué número de la calle Mayor está la frutería?
24 ¿Dónde está el metro?
25 ¿Dónde hay una zapatería?

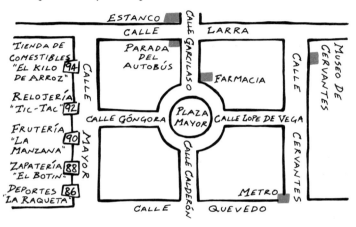

AT THE HOTEL

You want a double room, with a double bed and sea views:
26 _____

¿Para cuántas noches?
You want to stay five nights.
27 _____

¿Tiene equipaje?
Say: 'Yes, these four suitcases':
28 _____

Now ask how much it is per night:
29 _____

ASKING FOR A SINGLE ROOM

You want a single room, with a bathroom:
30 _____

Muy bien. ¿Para cuántas noches?
You want it for three nights:
31 _____
Muy bien.
Ask at what time they serve breakfast:
32 _____

TRANSLATE INTO SPANISH

33 Can I smoke in the cafeteria?
34 Can I park in this square?
35 Can I visit the cathedral?
36 Can I go by tube?
37 Can I book a room?

WORTH KNOWING

BY TUBE AND BUS

There are good bus services in the cities, and also a fast and reliable tube service in Madrid, Barcelona and Valencia. There is a fixed price for all destinations, and you can get *un bono* (a pass), with considerable savings. The 'bus pass' is called *un bonobús.*

BY TAXI

Taxis may not have a glass divider between the driver and the passenger, therefore contact is close and it's natural to have a conversation. Taxis will charge you extras like:

la bajada de bandera initial amount
la salida de estación extra for waiting at a station

When a taxi is available, the word *libre* (free) is displayed at the top corner of the windscreen. At night they have a green light. Tip the driver with 5 or 10 per cent of the total fare. You can also ask the driver to keep the change: *Quédese con la vuelta.*

OFFICE HOURS – *EL HORARIO COMERCIAL*

Government departments, banks and private companies are open from 9.00 a.m. to 2.00 p.m. (or *la jornada intensiva*). Shops, travel agents, etc. are generally open from around 9.00 a.m. to 1.30 p.m. and then from 4.00 p.m. to about 7.30 p.m. (or *la jornada partida*). Museums may remain open all day long. Larger department stores are open all day. During the summer months some companies and shops have different opening hours.

TO PHONE ABROAD

Dial 07, wait for the tone to change, and then dial the British STD code (or any other country's prefixed code) followed by the number you want. You should be able to use any coins. Don't forget that Spain is one hour ahead in relation to Britain!

You can phone from *un teléfono interurbano* (phone box for international calls). Or go to *Teléfonos* – a telephone service facility with several booths, each with a meter. You pay the receptionist once you've finished your call. You will find a *Teléfonos* in most resorts. Just ask: *¿Dónde está Teléfonos?*

HOTELS

There are nearly a million hotel beds, and more than 10 000 establishments of different types in Spain. Spanish hotels rate from one star to the five star luxury establishment, and *los hostales* (inexpensive and simple hotels) range from one to three stars. As well as *los hoteles, los hostales* and *las pensiones* (B&Bs), there are the so-called *paradores,* which are mostly places of historic and artistic interest that have been converted into reasonably priced hotels. The 86 Spanish *paradores* are state owned, and many of them were once convents, castles or palaces. They promote local food and wine.

You may find that breakfast is not included in the accommodation price, specially in the more expensive hotels. Look out for *media pensión* (half board) and *pensión completa* (full board).

4 GETTING TO YOUR DESTINATION

KEY WORDS AND PHRASES

alquilar	to rent
el coche	car
un coche de cuatro puertas	a four-door car
¿Cuánto cuesta?	How much does it cost?
un kilómetro	a kilometre
quiero ir a . . .	I want to go to . . .
un billete de ida	a single ticket
un billete de ida y vuelta	a return ticket
¿Cuánto dura el viaje?	How long does the journey last?
que sale . . .	that leaves . . .
y luego ya . . .	and then . . .
solamente lleva camas	just has sleeping compartments
¿A qué hora sale el avión para . . . ?	What time does the plane for . . . leave?
¿A qué hora llega a . . . ?	What time does it arrive at . . . ?
quiero un billete para . . .	I want a ticket for . . .
¿Cuándo quiere ir?	When do you want to go?
una plaza libre	an available seat/place
¿Cómo va a pagar?	How are you going to pay?
con tarjeta	by credit card
en efectivo	by cash

CONVERSATIONS

RENTING A CAR

ISABEL   Buenos días. Quiero[1] alquilar un coche para una semana. ¿Cuánto cuesta?

EMPLEADA   Buenos días. Mire, uno de cuatro puertas, cinco mil seiscientas pesetas el día, y cuarenta y nueve pesetas el kilómetro.

ISABEL   ¿Y de dos puertas?

EMPLEADA   De dos puertas, tres mil novecientas pesetas el día, y veintinueve pesetas el kilómetro.

AT THE TRAVEL AGENCY

ISABEL   Buenos días, quiero ir a Barcelona. ¿Cómo puedo ir?

EMPLEADA   Puede ir en tren, en autocar o en avión con el puente aéreo.

ISABEL   ¿Cuánto cuesta ir en autocar hasta Barcelona?

EMPLEADA   En autocar cuesta cuatro mil quinientas pesetas.

ISABEL   ¿Ida y vuelta?

EMPLEADA   Sí, ida y vuelta.

ISABEL   ¿Y en tren?

EMPLEADA   En tren cuesta doce mil trescientas cincuenta pesetas, ida y vuelta.

ISABEL   ¿Y en avión?

EMPLEADA   En avión, con el puente aéreo, veintidós mil quinientas pesetas.

HOW LONG IS THE JOURNEY?

ISABEL   ¿Cuánto dura el viaje?

EMPLEADA   El viaje en autocar dura nueve horas, en tren ocho horas y en el puente aéreo cuarenta y cinco minutos.

WHAT TRAINS ARE THERE TO BARCELONA?

ISABEL	¿Qué trenes hay para Barcelona, por favor?
EMPLEADA	El Expreso . . . Expreso 'Estrella – Costa Brava', que sale a las veintiuna cuarenta.
	Después tiene el Expreso 'Ciudad Condal', que sale a las veintidós treinta.
	Y luego ya un Talgo, que solamente lleva camas.
ISABEL	¿Qué precio tiene el Talgo, por favor?
EMPLEADA	El doble, ocho mil seiscientas y el individual, trece mil doscientas.

ARRIVAL AND DEPARTURE TIMES

PABLO	Oiga, perdone. ¿A qué hora sale el avión para Londres?
EMPLEADO	A las diecisiete cero cinco.
PABLO	¿Y a qué hora llega a Londres?
EMPLEADO	Bueno, llega a las dieciocho horas, hora local.

GETTING A PLANE TICKET

PABLO	Quiero un billete para Londres.
EMPLEADA	¿De ida o de ida y vuelta?
PABLO	De ida y vuelta.
EMPLEADA	¿Cuándo quiere ir?
PABLO	El sábado, 18 de mayo.
EMPLEADA	¿Y volver?
PABLO	Una semana después, el 25, también sábado.
EMPLEADA	Muy bien . . . pues sí, hay una plaza libre.
PABLO	Ah, estupendo. ¿Cuánto cuesta?
EMPLEADA	Son veintiocho mil veintisiete pesetas. ¿Cómo va a pagar? ¿Con tarjeta o en efectivo?
PABLO	En efectivo. Aquí tiene, cinco mil, diez mil, quince mil, veinte mil . . .

WORD LIST

después	afterwards, later
en autocar	by coach
en avión	by plane
en barco	by boat
en tren	by train
hasta	to, as far as, until
la hora local	local time
mayo	May
el puente aéreo	shuttle service (by air)
pues	well, well then
sábado	Saturday
una semana	a week
el viaje	journey, trip
volver	to come back, return

EXPLANATIONS

WANTING TO DO SOMETHING

If you want to rent a car or an apartment you use:

Quiero alquilar . . .

EXAMPLES:

Quiero alquilar un coche

Quiero alquilar un apartamento (an apartment or flat)

Quiero alquilar una bicicleta (a bicycle)

Quiero alquilar una casa (de tres habitaciones) (three bedroomed house)

You'll be asked: 'How long for?' *¿Para cuánto tiempo?* and can reply:

Para un día For one day

Para un par de días For a couple of days

Para un mes For one month

Para el mes de julio For the month of July

Para el verano For the summer
And when you're told the price, don't forget that if it's *todo incluído* it means there will be no hidden extras. It might be wise to ask *¿Todo incluído?*

When you want to go somewhere use: *Quiero ir a . . .*
EXAMPLES:
Quiero ir a Madrid
Quiero ir a la Alhambra
Quiero ir al Hotel Alfonso XIII
(NOTE THAT YOU DO NOT SAY *A EL,* BUT *AL.*)

HOW MUCH DOES IT COST?

Another way to ask the price of something is to use:
¿Cuánto cuesta?
EXAMPLES:
¿Cuánto cuesta el billete? How much does the ticket cost?
¿Cuánto cuesta el pasaje? How much does the fare (for ship and plane) cost?
¿Cuánto cuesta la entrada? How much does the ticket (for cinema/shows) cost?
¿Cuánto cuesta el ticket/billete? How much does the ticket (for transport) cost?
¿Cuánto cuesta en primera? How much does first class cost?
¿Cuánto cuesta en segunda? How much does second class cost?

Use *¿Cuánto cuestan?* for plurals.
EXAMPLE:
¿Cuánto cuestan los billetes?

HOW LONG DOES IT TAKE?

To ask how long a journey takes use:
¿Cuánto dura?
EXAMPLES:
¿Cuánto dura el viaje? How long does the journey take?

¿Cuánto dura el vuelo? How long does the flight take?
¿Cuánto dura la travesía? How long does the crossing take?
¿Cuánto dura la gira? How long does the tour take?
¿Cuánto dura la película? How long does the film last?

REPLIES:
de tres a seis de la tarde from 3 p.m. to 6 p.m.
un cuarto de hora a quarter of an hour
unas dos horas about two hours
tres horas y media three and a half hours
dos horas y tres cuartos two and three quarter hours
una hora y cuarto an hour and a quarter
toda la noche all night
todo el día all day

DEPARTURES AND ARRIVALS

To ask when your train leaves say:
¿A qué hora sale el tren?
Or when your plane takes off:
¿A qué hora sale el avión para Madrid?
To find out when the train arrives at your destination:
¿A qué hora llega el tren a Barcelona?
REPLIES:
A las tres de la tarde. A medianoche

THE TWENTY-FOUR HOUR CLOCK

At a station or airport times of departure and arrival are
usually announced using the twenty-four hour clock:
EXAMPLES:
19.35 *las diecinueve treinta y cinco*
13.30 *las trece treinta*
06.05 *las seis cero cinco*
20.00 *las veinte horas*
11.55 *las once cincuenta y cinco*
14.10 *las catorce diez*

WHEN DO YOU WANT TO GO?

You'll be asked when you want to go:

¿Cuándo quiere ir?

REPLIES:

el veinte de agosto the 20th of August

esta tarde this afternoon

mañana tomorrow

Then when do you want to return:

¿Cuándo quiere volver?

REPLIES:

un mes después a month later

el diez de septiembre the 10th of September

(DAYS OF THE WEEK, MONTHS OF THE YEAR AND HOW TO SAY THE
DATE CAN ALL BE FOUND IN THE REFERENCE SECTiON.)

7 PAYING

You'll be asked how you are going to pay:

¿Cómo va a pagar?

REPLIES:

en efectivo by cash   *con cheque* by cheque

con tarjeta by credit card   *a plazos* in instalments

ATTRACTING SOMEONE'S ATTENTION

¡Oiga! Excuse me!

¡Oiga, perdone! Excuse me! (more polite)

¡Oiga, por favor! Excuse me, please!

EXERCISES

RENTING A CAR

You want to rent a four-door car. Start off by saying 'Good
morning':

1 _____

¿Para cuánto tiempo?

You reply: 'For a month':
2 _____
Muy bien.

AT THE TRAVEL AGENT'S

Say that you want to go to Mallorca:
3 _____
Puede ir en avión o en barco.
Say that you want to go by ship:
4 _____
Ask how long the journey takes:
5 _____
Nueve horas, de diez de la noche a siete de la mañana.
Say that you want a single ticket:
6 _____

AT THE RAILWAY STATION

Ask about trains to Bilbao:
7 _____
Hay uno esta noche.
Enquire about the price:
8 _____
Son cinco mil setecientas, ida y vuelta.
Say that you want two return tickets:
9 _____

TRANSLATE INTO SPANISH

10 At what time does the train leave?
11 At what time does the plane arrive?
12 How much does it cost to go to Valencia by train?
13 How long does the flight take?
14 Is there a train to Zaragoza today?
15 I want to rent a flat in August (for the month of August).
16 How much does the Express cost?

FILL IN THE GAPS

17   Getting a one-way plane ticket to London:

SEÑOR   Buenos _____ . _____ un billete de
             _____ para _____ .

EMPLEADO   Hola, _____ días. ¿Cuándo _____ ir?

SEÑOR   _____ veintinueve _____ julio.

EMPLEADO   ¿Y_____ ?

SEÑOR   _____ semana _____ . El cinco de
             _____ .

EMPLEADO   Muy _____ .

SEÑOR   ¿Cuánto dura el _____ ?

EMPLEADO   Una hora y _____ cuartos. ¿Cómo _____ .
             a pagar?

SEÑOR   En _____ . ¿A qué _____ sale?

EMPLEADO   A _____ once de _____ mañana.

SEÑOR   ¿Y a _____ hora _____ ?

EMPLEADO   _____ las _____ _____ _____
             _____ (11.45), hora local.

WORTH KNOWING

BY CAR

If you take your own car to Spain, there are a few rules you have to comply with. First of all, it would be advisable to have an international driving licence. Concerning insurance, it is compulsory to have a 'green card', which is provided when you extend your insurance cover. You must also take:

- a triangle reflector, in case your car breaks down
- a beam reflector
- spare light bulbs

Seat belts are compulsory, as in many European countries. By the way, if you're driving through France, you're required to take your vehicle registration documents as proof of ownership.

MOTORING VOCABULARY

el permiso de conducir driving licence
el taller de reparaciones garage, workshop
el garaje private parking garage
el aparcamiento/el parking car park
el parquímetro parking metre
la gasolina petrol
la gasalina sin plomo unleaded petrol
la gasolinera/la estación de servicio service station
Se ha pinchado la rueda I've got a flat tyre
limpiar el coche to clean the car

When something's not working properly, you can say *no funciona* (it's not working):
No funciona el coche The car isn't working
No funciona el embrague The clutch isn't working
No funciona la caja de cambios The gear box isn't working

ROADS AND MOTORWAYS

There's an excellent network of motorways and main roads linking cities and towns in Spain. On some motorways you will have to pay a toll (*un peaje.*)
On maps, remember that:

- A – stands for *autopista,* or motorway
- N – stands for *carretera nacional,* or main road
- C – stands for *comarcal,* or secondary road

BY TRAIN

RENFE is the national railway company, and it stands for *Red Nacional de Ferrocarriles Españoles.*

For reductions on regular rates, you can buy a *chequetrén* (15 per cent discount on fares). You can also travel on certain dates (*días azules* or blue days!), which are off-peak and allow for lower prices.

TRAINS:
el Talgo/el Intercity luxury trains/Intercity
el tren de cercanías commuter, local train
el Expreso night train
REMEMBER:
El tren con destino a . . . The train to . . .
El tren procedente de . . . The train from . . .

BY COACH

There are excellent coach services throughout Spain. For more information you should contact a local travel agent.

BY PLANE

Spanish airlines have flights to most countries, and there are airports in major Spanish cities. The shuttle service between Madrid and Barcelona is called *el puente aéreo* (literally 'air bridge'), and there's a flight every hour. Check the phone directory for information on Spanish airline services.

TO LET/FOR SALE

You will see these signs displayed in flats, holiday apartments, boats, etc. when they're for hire or for sale:
Se alquila To let
Se vende For sale

5 LIVING IN SPAIN

KEY WORDS AND PHRASES

Te presento a . . .	May I introduce you to . . . ?
encantado/a	delighted to meet you
mucho gusto	it's a pleasure
¿De dónde es usted?	Where are you from?
¿En qué ciudad vive?	Which city do you live in?
vivo en . . .	I live in . . .
casado/a	married
soltero/a	single
¿Cuántos hijos tiene?	How many children do you have?
¿Cuántos años tiene usted?	How old are you?
¿Qué profesión tiene usted?	What's your profession/job?
¿Dónde trabaja usted?	Where do you work?
Español/a	Spanish person
¿Dónde ha nacido?	Where were you born?
¿Qué idiomas habla usted?	What languages do you speak?
hablo inglés	I speak English
¿A qué hora desayuna/come/ cena?	What time do you have breakfast/ lunch/dinner?
¿Cuál es el menú del día?	What's the set menu?
para mí, lo mismo	the same for me
yo prefiero	I prefer
la cuenta	the bill
quédese con la vuelta	keep the change

CONVERSATIONS

INTRODUCTIONS

RAQUEL   Felisa, te presento a Pepe, mi marido.
FELISA   Encantada.
PEPE   ¿Qué tal? Mucho gusto.

WHERE ARE YOU FROM?

ISABEL   ¿De dónde es usted?
Dª JULIA   Soy de Burgos.
ISABEL   ¿Y en qué ciudad vive?
Dª JULIA   Ahora vivo en Madrid.
ISABEL   ¿En qué zona de Madrid?
Dª JULIA   En la zona norte.

MARRIED? ANY CHILDREN?

ISABEL   ¿Es usted casada o soltera?
RAQUEL   Casada.
ISABEL   ¿Cuántos hijos tiene?
RAQUEL   Diez.
ISABEL   ¿Tiene usted diez hijos?
RAQUEL   Sí, diez hijos.

HOW OLD ARE YOU?

ISABEL   ¿Cuántos años tiene usted?
CARLOS   Treinta y tres.

WHAT DO YOU DO FOR A LIVING?

ISABEL   ¿Qué profesión tiene usted?
CARLOS   Comercio.
ISABEL   ¿Qué tipo de comercio?
CARLOS   De automóviles.
ISABEL   ¿Vende usted automóviles?
CARLOS   Sí, si puedo . . .

WHERE DO YOU WORK?

ISABEL ¿Dónde trabaja usted?

MONTSE En un banco.

ISABEL ¿Le gusta su trabajo?

MONTSE Sí, me gusta mucho. Es muy interesante.

WHAT'S YOUR NATIONALITY?

ISABEL ¿Qué nacionalidad tiene usted?

CARLOS Soy español.

ISABEL ¿Y dónde ha nacido?

CARLOS En Pozuelo de Alarcón, de Madrid.

WHAT LANGUAGES DO YOU SPEAK?

ISABEL ¿Qué idiomas habla usted?

SUSANA Hablo inglés . . .

ISABEL ¿Nada más?

SUSANA Y un poco de francés.

WHAT TIME DO YOU HAVE YOUR MEALS?

ISABEL ¿A qué hora desayuna?

RAQUEL A las ocho.

ISABEL ¿A qué hora come?

RAQUEL A las dos y media o tres.

ISABEL ¿A qué hora cena?

RAQUEL A las diez.

ORDERING A MEAL

ISABEL Camarero, por favor. ¿Cuál es el menú del día?

CAMARERO De primero, hay gazpacho o sopa. Y de segundo, hay merluza a la romana o cordero asado.

ISABEL De primero, gazpacho, y de segundo, merluza.

ANA Y para mí, lo mismo.

ISABEL	Y de postre, ¿qué tienen?
CAMARERO	Hay helado, natillas, arroz con leche, piña, melocotón . . .
ISABEL	Melocotón, por favor.
ANA	Yo prefiero piña.
CAMARERO	Muy bien. ¿Y para beber?
ISABEL	Vino blanco.
ANA	Sí. El vino de la casa, por favor.

HOW'S THE FOOD?

CAMARERO	¿Qué tal el gazpacho?
ISABEL	Está muy bueno.
CAMARERO	¿Y la merluza?
ANA	¡Está buenísima!
CAMARERO	¿Y el vino?
ISABEL	¿El vino? . . . El vino no está mal.

PAYING THE BILL

ISABEL	¿Me puede dar la cuenta, por favor?
CAMARERO	Sí, ahora mismo.
ISABEL	¿Cuánto es en total?
CAMARERO	Mil setecientas treinta.
ISABEL	Aquí tiene, dos mil. Quédese con la vuelta. Muchas gracias.
CAMARERO	A usted señora. Gracias.
ISABEL	De nada. Adiós.
ANA	Adiós.

WORD LIST

ahora mismo	right now, immediately
un año	a year
el automóvil	car
buenísimo/a	extremely good
el comercio	business (usually sales)
de postre	for dessert
de primero/segundo	for first/second course
el francés	French (language)
los hijos	children
interesante	interesting
mal	bad, badly
el marido	husband
la nacionalidad	nationality
norte	north
la profesión	profession, occupation
si puedo	if I can
Soy de . . .	I'm from . . .
su	your (formal), his, her, its
el trabajo	work, job
el vino de la casa	house wine
la zona	area, district
Soy español	I'm Spanish

EXPLANATIONS

INTRODUCTIONS

Te presento a . . . (informal)
Le presento a . . . (formal)

REPLIES:

Encantada/encantado I'm delighted
Mucho gusto It's a pleasure
¿Qué tal? How do you do?

WHERE ARE YOU FROM?

The way to ask where someone comes from is:

¿De dónde es (usted)? (formal)

¿De dónde eres (tú)? (informal)

REPLIES:

Soy de Madrid

Soy de Colombia

Soy de Inglaterra (England)

Soy de Gran Bretaña (Great Britain)

Soy de Estados Unidos (United States)

WHERE DO YOU LIVE?

You can ask a general question:

¿Dónde vive (usted)? (formal)

¿Dónde vives (tú)? (informal)

To which the reply is:

Vivo en España

Vivo en Birmingham

Or you can ask which town or city people live in:

¿En qué ciudad vive (usted)?

¿En qué ciudad vives (tú)?

Vivo en Madrid

Vivo en Londres (London)

Vivo en Nueva York (New York)

And in which area or district:

¿En qué zona de Barcelona?

REPLIES:

Vivo en la zona norte I live in the north

Vivo en la zona sur I live in the south

Vivo en la zona este I live in the east

Vivo en la zona oeste I live in the west

Vivo en el barrio gótico I live in the Gothic quarter

Or you can also say

Vivo al norte   Vivo al sur   Vivo al este   Vivo al oeste

NATIONALITY

You might, in an official situation, be asked your nationality:
¿Qué nacionalidad tiene usted?

REPLY:

Soy de Gran Bretaña
Soy de Estados Unidos
Soy británico/a (British)
Soy norteamericano/a (North American)
Soy australiano/a (Australian)

Or you might be asked where you were born:
¿Dónde ha nacido usted?

REPLY:

He nacido en Bristol I was born in Bristol

HOW OLD ARE YOU?

There are two ways to ask this question:
¿Cuántos años tiene (usted)? (formal)
¿Cuántos años tienes (tú)? (informal)

REPLY:

Tengo treinta y ocho años

WHAT DO YOU DO?

To find out someone's profession ask:
¿Qué profesión tiene usted?

REPLIES:

Soy contable I'm an accountant
Soy profesor/a I'm a teacher
Soy enfermero/a I'm a nurse
Soy hombre/mujer de negocios I'm a business man/woman

To ask where someone works:
¿Dónde trabaja (usted)? or *¿Dónde trabajas (tú)?*

REPLIES:

en un banco	*en un hospital*
en un colegio (a school)	*en una oficina* (an office)

TENER
....

You'll have noticed (and used) *tener* throughout this course. It doesn't just mean 'to have'; it's also used in expressions about price, age, profession and nationality. The endings change for each person:

EXAMPLES:

Formal 'you':

¿Tiene usted hijos? Have you got any children?

¿Cuántos hijos tiene? How many children have you got?

Informal 'you':

¿Tienes un diccionario? Have you got a dictionary?

¿Tienes fuego? Have you got a light?

'It'/'he'/'she':

¿Qué precio tiene este jamón? How much is this ham?

Lola tiene treinta años Lola is 30 years old

'I':

Tengo dolor de estómago I've got stomach ache

No tengo hijos I haven't got any children

'We':

Tenemos pollo, tortilla . . . We've got chicken, omelette . . .

No tenemos pescado hay. We don't have any fish today.

'They':

¿Qué precio tienen estos pantalones? How much are these trousers?

Mis padres tienen un coche roja. My parents have a red car.

Other useful expressions with *tener*:

Tengo sed I'm thirsty

Tengo hambre I'm hungry

Tengo sueño I'm sleepy

Tengo calor I'm hot

Tengo frío I'm cold

TO LIKE DOING SOMETHING

To say you like doing something use *me gusta* and a verb:

EXAMPLES:

Me gusta visitar castillos

Me gusta hablar español

To ask if someone likes doing something use *¿le gusta?* for the formal and *¿te gusta?* for the informal:

EXAMPLES:

¿Le gusta hablar español?

¿Te gusta viajar? (to travel)

Asking where someone likes to go, add *¿Dónde . . . ?*:

¿Dónde le/te gusta ir de vacaciones? Where do you like to go on holiday?

REPLIES:

Me gusta ir a un camping (to a campsite)

Me gusta ir al campo (to the country)

Me gusta ir a la montaña (to the mountains)

Me gusta ir a la playa (to the seaside/beach)

And asking 'why?':

¿Por qué le/te gusta ir a la montaña? Why do you like to go to the mountains?

Porque me gusta esquiar Because I like skiing

ORDERING A MEAL

A three-course meal in Spain consists of:

el primer plato the first course

el segundo plato the second course

el postre the dessert

To ask the waiter what's on the menu use *¿Qué hay . . . ?*

¿Qué hay de primero?

¿Qué hay de segundo?

¿Qué hay de postre?

¿Qué hay para comer?

¿Qué hay para beber?

You can also ask:
¿Qué tienen de primero?

Here are some typical Spanish dishes:

DE PRIMERO:	STARTER
ensalada (f.)	salad
entremeses (m.)	hors d'œuvres
sopa (f.)	soup
gazpacho (m.)	gazpacho (cold tomato-based soup)
consomé (m.)	consommé
potaje (m.)	vegetable stew
paella (f.)	paella (rice with seafood and chicken)

DE SEGUNDO:	MAIN COURSE
merluza a la romana (f.)	fried hake
cordero asado (m.)	roast lamb
pollo (m.)	chicken
solomillo (m.)	sirloin steak
entrecot (m.)	entrecôte steak
tortilla española (f.)	Spanish omelette

DE POSTRE:	DESSERT
helado (m.)	ice-cream
arroz con leche (m.)	rice pudding
natillas (f.)	custard
piña (f.)	pineapple (fresh or tinned)
melocotón (m.)	peach (fresh or tinned)
fruta del tiempo (f.)	fresh fruit
flan (m.)	creme caramel

When you want the waiter to give you the menu:
¿Me puede dar la carta?

WHAT'S THE FOOD LIKE?

EXAMPLES:
¿Qué tal la comida? or *¿Qué tal está la comida?*
¿Qué tal el vino?

REPLIES:
Está muy buena/o It's very good
Está buenísima/o It's extremely good
No está mal It's not bad

PAYING THE BILL

¿Me puede dar la cuenta, por favor? or
La cuenta, por favor May I have the bill please?
To give a tip, say:
Quédese con la vuelta Keep the change

RELATIONS AND FRIENDS

el abuelo/la abuela	grandfather/grandmother
la esposa/mujer	wife
el esposo/marido	husband
la madre/el padre	mother/father
el hijo/la hija	son/daughter
el hermano/la hermana	brother/sister
el amigo/la amiga	male friend/female friend

For mixed groups use the masculine plural:

los padres	parents
los abuelos	grandparents
los hijos	children
los amigos	friends

EXERCISES

A CONVERSATION

You're having a conversation with a Spanish man. Begin by
asking what his name is (use the formal throughout):

1 _____

Me llamo Vicente Gómez Garcés.
Now ask where he's from:
2 _____
Soy de Lugo.
Now ask him if he's married or single:
3 _____
Casado.
Ask him what his occupation is:
4 _____
Soy profesor de inglés.
Ask him which city he lives in:
5 _____
En Madrid.
And ask in what area:
6 _____
En la zona sur de Madrid.

IN A RESTAURANT

Call the waiter:
7 _____
¿Qué va a tomar?
Ask what there is for first course:
8 _____
Gazpacho o consomé.
Now ask what there is for second course:
9 _____
Merluza o cordero asado.
And now ask what there is for dessert:
10 _____
Natillas o helado.
Say you want cold tomato soup, hake and ice-cream:
11 _____

THE BILL, PLEASE

Ask the waiter for the bill:

12 _____

Sí. Son novecientas diez pesetas.

Give him a thousand pesetas, and tell him to keep the change:

13 _____

FILL IN THE GAPS

14 CARLOS   ¿ _____ tal el vino?

    FELISA   _____ muy bueno.

    CARLOS   ¿Le _____ la paella?

    FELISA   _____ gusta muchísimo.

15 MIGUEL   ¿ _____ hay de primero?

   CAMARERO   _____ consomé o gazpacho.

    MIGUEL   ¿Y de _____ ?

   CAMARERO   Hay merluza _____ pollo.

    MIGUEL   ¿Y _____ postre?

   CAMARERO   Hay flan, _____ del tiempo o arroz con leche.

WORTH KNOWING

SPAIN – _ESPAÑA_

Spain is a land of contrasts. The extraordinary changes from one region to the next in everything from scenery to folklore and from cuisine to customs are obviously an indication that the country has been influenced over the ages by diverse cultures and peoples. Ranking eleventh among the world's main industrialised countries, Spain has become a unique combination of European advancement and centuries–old traditions. Some say that such uniqueness is because 'Spain is different' . . . _¡España es diferente!_

SPANISH – *EL ESPAÑOL*

Spanish is a language which is extensively spoken. It's actually one of the main languages worldwide and there are more than 300 million people whose mother tongue is Spanish. If you consider that people speak Spanish not only in Spain and most of Latin America but also in the United States, where there's a large Spanish-speaking community, you'll realise that you're now learning an important and extremely useful language indeed.

Spanish, *el español* is also known as Castilian *(el castellano)*, because it's the language which originated from *Castilla* or Castile, the central region in Spain. You'll find that in some parts of Spain people speak another language besides Spanish:
el catalán (Catalan), in Catalonia
el gallego (Galician), in Galicia (northwest Spain)
el vasco (Basque), in the Basque Country

SPANISH COOKING – *LA COCINA ESPAÑOLA*

Spanish regional cuisine is extremely varied: the Basque country and Galicia are famous for fish dishes; Catalonia, for casseroles; Levante, for paella and seafood dishes; Andalusia, for fried foods; and central Spain, for roasts. Visitors should expect excellent quality as well as quantity, as the amounts served are usually more than generous.

RESTAURANTS – *LOS RESTAURANTES*

Restaurants will usually offer a menu (*la carta*) and a set menu (*el menú del día*). The *menú del día* includes a first course, second course, bread, wine and either dessert or coffee. For any additional item, you'll have to pay extra (*un suplemento*).

If you want a quick lunch in a cafeteria you can have *un plato combinado,* which is a two-course meal, including wine, bread and dessert. Alternatively, if you're not very hungry, you could just have *un bocadillo,* a roll of bread filled with anything you like (omelette, cheese, cooked ham, Serrano ham, chorizo, even squid). For traditional Spanish dishes and atmosphere eat at *un mesón,* a typical eating and drinking place.

If you want to lodge a complaint against a restaurant, you can ask the owner or manager for *las hojas de reclamaciones* (complaints forms).

EATING AT HOME

Spaniards enjoy food considerably, and they usually have two large meals a day, plus several 'in-betweens'. The average Spaniard starts the day with a light breakfast, *el desayuno.* There may also be a mid-morning snack. Lunch, *el almuerzo* or *la comida,* is followed by a mid-afternoon snack, *la merienda* (equivalent to the British tea). And, of course, there is a very late supper, *la cena.*

A main meal will usually include two courses, followed by dessert, coffee, and sometimes a liqueur, like *el coñac* (brandy) or *el anís* (anisette).

REMEMBER:
desayunar to have breakfast
almorzar to have a light lunch or a mid-morning snack
comer to have lunch/dinner
merendar to have tea
cenar to have supper

Spaniards are well known for their hospitality, and they will go to great lengths in order to make their guests enjoy the meal they've prepared. If you're invited to dinner, take perhaps flowers, a cake, some chocolates or a small present, but never a bottle of wine, unless you've been asked to do so. As Spaniards normally drink wine with their food, drinks are always provided by your host, who will obviously choose what best suits the menu.

Be prepared to stay on at the table once the meal is finished, over coffee and perhaps a liqueur. This is what Spaniards call *la sobremesa,* and it's a chance to chat and relax for a while after a hearty meal. If the weather's too hot, you can even lie down for a nap or *una siesta.* And in the evening, dress up smartly and go for *el paseo* or walk, in the main city square or in the main streets (most towns have a *Plaza Mayor,* and a *calle Mayor*). You can also sit down for a drink and some *tapas* in a bar, just watching people go by . . . until supper time at ten o'clock!

Enjoy your stay in Spain!

CAN YOU GET BY?

This is a final set of exercises to test your knowledge of Spanish at the end of the course.

WHERE WOULD YOU BUY WHAT?

1 unos zapatos
2 una camisa
3 un sello
4 un kilo de pollo
5 medio kilo de uvas
6 una barra de pan
7 un libro
8 un billete de avión

a una panadería
b un estanco
c una agencia de viajes
d una zapatería
e una pollería
f una camisería
g una frutería
h una librería

CHOOSE THE CORRECT ANSWER

9 ¿Se puede fumar?
10 ¿Dónde están los lavabos?
11 ¿Cuánto dura el viaje en avión?
12 ¿Dónde ha nacido usted?
13 ¿Cómo se llama su marido?
14 ¿Qué va a tomar de primero?
15 ¿Cuánto cuesta alquilar un apartamento de dos habitaciones?

16   ¿En qué puedo servirle?
17   ¿Tiene algo para la indigestión?
18   ¿Qué hora es?

a   Quiero un kilo y medio de manzanas.
b   Aproximadamente una hora y media.
c   No, ésta es la zona de no fumadores.
d   José García López.
e   Veinte mil a la semana, y setenta y cinco mil al mes.
f   Son las diez menos cuarto.
g   La primera puerta a la derecha.
h   Estas pastillas son muy buenas.
i   En Barcelona.
j   Un gazpacho.

WRITE THE FOLLOWING NUMBERS IN SPANISH

19 1001 ● **20** 88 ● **21** 69 ● **22** 375 ● **23** 7.5
24 12.360 ● **25** 0.2 ● **26** 15% ● **27** 1.750.825 pesetas
28 1.999 pesetas

TRANSLATE THE FOLLOWING

29   Where are the toilets?
30   I want a pair of shoes.
31   I don't like (the) brown trousers.
32   I want to go to the beach.
33   Today's the 15th of December.
34   May I help you?
35   How old are you? (informal)
36   How much is the plane ticket?
37   I speak a little Spanish.
38   I'm British, and I'm in Spain on holiday.

FILL IN THE GAPS

39   An official conversation

EMPLEADO	Buenas _____ . ¿Cómo _____ llama _____ ?
CLIENTE	_____ tardes. Me _____ Peter.
EMPLEADO	¿Y de _____ ?
CLIENTE	Robinson.
EMPLEADO	¿ _____ ha nacido _____ ?
CLIENTE	En Gran Bretaña. Soy _____ .
EMPLEADO	¿En qué _____ vive _____ ?
CLIENTE	_____ en Londres.
EMPLEADO	¿ _____ usted _____ o _____ ?
CLIENTE	Casado.

REFERENCE SECTION

PRONUNCIATION GUIDE

Sounds are very difficult to convey on a written page, so you should use this section in close conjunction with the audio cassette recordings at the beginning of Side 1 of Cassette 1.

THE STRESS OR 'ACCENT' – *EL ACENTO*

Words of more than one syllable which end in a vowel, *n* or *s* are stressed on the last but one syllable:
Es<u>pa</u>ña ● *to<u>ma</u>te* ● *impo<u>si</u>ble* ● *<u>mu</u>cho* ● *<u>ca</u>lle* ● *te<u>ne</u>mos* ● *<u>co</u>men*

Words ending in a consonant other than *n* or *s*, are stressed on the last syllable:
co<u>mer</u> ● *espa<u>ñol</u>* ● *ciu<u>dad</u>*

In other cases, the written accent tells you where the stress is:
pantalón ● *kilómetro* ● *inglés* ● *menú* ● *plátano* ●

Sometimes the accent indicates a different meaning:

sí	yes	*si*	if
sólo	only	*solo*	alone
éste	this one	*este*	this
él	he	*el*	the (masculine, singular)

NOTE: CAPITAL LETTERS ARE NOT USUALLY ACCENTED IN SPANISH.

VOWELS – *LAS VOCALES*

Spanish vowels are pronounced as distinctly and 'openly' as possible. There are five vowel sounds: *a e i o u*.
Try and say them out loud, following these indications:
a as in 'hut' (standard English) *gracias*
e as in 'get' *este*   *o* as in 'lot' *color*
i as in 'heed' *imposible*   *u* as in 'mood' *azul*

CONSONANTS – *LAS CONSONANTES*

b/v   are both pronounced as a 'b':
        at the beginning of a word, as in 'boy' *barco, vino*
        in the middle of a word, they are softer *abuelo, avión*
c   before *a, o, u* and *r* as 'k' *casa, comida, cristal*
        before *e* and *i*, a 'th' sound as in 'thin' *cero, ciudad*
ch   is a separate letter in Spanish and pronounced as in English *mucho*
d   as in English, but softer. After a vowel, or an *r* or at the end of a word, a 'th' sound as in '*then*' *donde, Madrid, Córdoba*
f   as in English *francés*
g   before *i* and *e* a 'ch' sound as in the Scottish 'loch' *gira*
        before *a, o, u*, or consonant and before *ue, ui* (the *u* is NOT pronounced unless it has a dieresis: *pingüino*) as in 'game', but softer   *gustar, grande, guitarra*
j   before all vowels a 'ch' sound as in Scottish 'loch' *jamón, junio*
h   it is always silent *hotel*
k   as in English *kilo*
l   as in English *Lola*
ll   is a separate letter in Spanish and pronounced as a 'ye' sound *calle, Sevilla*
m   as in English *madre, mapa*
n   as in English *nada*
ñ   is pronounced 'ni' as in 'onion' *España*

p	as in English, but softer *pan, para*
q	used only with *ui* and *ue* as a 'k' sound (the *u* is NOT pronounced) *qué, quiero*
r	in the middle of a word is softly trilled *pero, caro*
r	at the beginning of a word and *rr* are doubly trilled *restaurante, barra*
s	less whistling than in English *solo, casa*
t	as in English, but softer *total*
x	as in English *exacto*
y	as in English, but stronger *yo*
z	is pronounced 'th' as in 'think' *zapato*

PUNCTUATION

¿ . . . ?, ¡ . . . !

In written Spanish you must always include an inverted question mark at the beginning of your question, and the same applies to exclamation marks:

¿Cómo estás? ¡Hola!

NUMBERS

0	*cero*	11	*once*	22	*veintidós*
1	*uno/a*	12	*doce*	23	*veintitrés*
2	*dos*	13	*trece*	24	*veinticuatro*
3	*tres*	14	*catorce*	25	*veinticinco*
4	*cuatro*	15	*quince*	26	*veintiséis*
5	*cinco*	16	*dieciséis*	27	*veintisiete*
6	*seis*	17	*diecisiete*	28	*veintiocho*
7	*siete*	18	*dieciocho*	29	*veintinueve*
8	*ocho*	19	*diecinueve*	30	*treinta*
9	*nueve*	20	*veinte*	31	*treinta y uno/a*
10	*diez*	21	*veintiuno/a*	32	*treinta y dos*
				33	*treinta y tres* etc.

(NOTE THAT AFTER 30, THE TWO NUMBERS ARE NOT JOINED INTO ONE WORD.)

40	*cuarenta*	300	*trescientos/as*
50	*cincuenta*	400	*cuatrocientos/as*
60	*sesenta*	500	*quinientos/as*
70	*setenta*	600	*seiscientos/as*
80	*ochenta*	700	*setecientos/as*
90	*noventa*	800	*ochocientos/as*
100	*cien*	900	*novecientos/as*
101	*ciento uno/a*	1000	*mil*
102	*ciento dos*	1 000 000	*un millón*
200	*doscientos/as*		

EXAMPLES:

99	*noventa y nueve*
157	*ciento cincuenta y siete*
379	*trescientos setenta y nueve*
1992	*mil novecientos noventa y dos*
3750	*tres mil setecientos cincuenta*
9999	*nueve mil novecientos noventa y nueve*

HOW MANY PESETAS?

Note that you must say *cuan**tas*** because it has to match *peset**as*** (feminine plural).

¿Cuántas pesetas?

REPLIES:

700 pesetas *setecien**tas** pesetas*

632 pesetas *seiscien**tas** treinta y dos pesetas*

350 000 pesetas *trescien**tas** cincuenta mil pesetas*

3.5 million pesetas *tres millones y medio de pesetas*

THOUSANDS

In Spanish a thousand is indicated with a full stop.

EXAMPLES: 1.000   30.000   1.000.000

DECIMALS

In Spanish, you use a comma for decimals.

EXAMPLE: one and a half or 1.5 is written 1,5 and spoken *uno coma cinco*.

PERCENTAGES

Per cent is *por ciento*.

EXAMPLES:

10% *diez por ciento*

25% *veinticinco por ciento*

a 20% discount *un veinte por ciento de descuento*

FIRST, SECOND, THIRD

1st	*primero/a*	or 1º (1ª)
2nd	*segundo/a*	or 2º (2ª)
3rd	*tercero/a*	or 3º (3ª)
4th	*cuarto/a*	or 4º (4ª)
5th	*quinto/a*	or 5º (5ª)
6th	*sexto/a*	or 6º (6ª)
7th	*séptimo/a*	or 7º (7ª)
8th	*octavo/a*	or 8º (8ª)
9th	*noveno/a*	or 9º (9ª)
10th	*décimo/a*	or 10º (10ª)

EXAMPLE:

La zapatería está en la tercera planta The shoe department is on the third floor

DAYS OF THE WEEK

lunes	Monday	*viernes*	Friday
martes	Tuesday	*sábado*	Saturday
miércoles	Wednesday	*domingo*	Sunday
jueves	Thursday		

MONTHS OF THE YEAR

enero	January	*julio*	July
febrero	February	*agosto*	August
marzo	March	*septiembre*	September
abril	April	*octubre*	October
mayo	May	*noviembre*	November
junio	June	*diciembre*	December

THE DATE

¿Qué día es hoy?	What's the date today?
Hoy es el siete de julio	It's the 7th of July today
El ocho de septiembre	8th of September
El once de abril	11th of April
El diecinueve de diciembre	19th of December
El primero/uno de marzo	1st of March

THE SEASONS

la primavera	spring	*el otoño*	autumn
el verano	summer	*el invierno*	winter

COLOURS

rojo/a	red	*gris*	grey
amarillo/a	yellow	*marrón*	brown
verde	green	*violeta*★	violet
azul	blue	*naranja*★	orange
negro/a	black	*rosa*★	pink
blanco/a	white		

(★NO CHANGE FOR MASCULINE/FEMININE AND SINGULAR/PLURAL.)

You can also say:

de color naranja orange   *de color negro* black

Light and dark:
claro/a light   *oscuro/a* dark

¿De qué color es/son . . . ? What colour is/are . . . ?
EXAMPLE:
¿De qué color es tu maleta? What colour is your suitcase?
Es roja It's red

THE WEATHER

Hace frío	It's cold
Hace calor	It's hot
Hace sol	It's sunny
Hace viento	It's windy
Está lloviendo/Llueve	It's raining
Está nevando/Nieva	It's snowing

MORE ADJECTIVES

alto/a	tall, high
antiguo/a	old (of things)
bajo/a	short, low
barato/a	cheap
caro/a	expensive
complicado/a	complicated
delgado/a	thin
difícil	difficult
divertido/a	funny
enorme	huge
estúpido/a	stupid
excelente	excellent
fácil	easy
fresco/a	cool
gracioso/a	amusing
grande	big
grueso/a	fat

horrible	horrible
imposible	impossible
inteligente	intelligent
interesante	interesting
joven	young
nuevo/a	new
pequeño/a	small
posible	possible
precioso/a	beautiful
privado/a	private
rico/a	delicious, rich
sabroso/a	tasty
salado/a	salty
simpático/a	nice, pleasant
simple	simple
viejo/a	old (of people)

YOU AND I

SUBJECT – I, YOU, HE, SHE, ETC.

yo	I
tú, usted	you
él, ella	he, she
nosotros/as	we
vosotros/as, ustedes	you
ellos, ellas	they

OBJECT – ME/TO ME, YOU/TO YOU, ETC.

me (a mí)	me, to me
te (a ti)	you, to you
lo/la, le (a él, a ella)	him/her, to him/her
nos (a nosotros)	us, to us
vos (a vosotros)	you, to you
los/las, les (a ellos)	them (masc. and fem.), to them

EXAMPLES:

¿Me quieres?	Do you love me?
Sí, te quiero	Yes, I love you
¿Te gusta este vino?	Do you like this wine?
No, no me gusta	No, I don't like it

FILLING IN A FORM

If you have to fill in a form (*un formulario, una ficha*) in Spain, you will probably have to provide the following information:

Nombre	Name
Apellidos	Surnames
Nacionalidad	Nationality
Dirección	Address
Ciudad	Town/city
País	Country
Teléfono	Telephone number
Profesión	Occupation
Sexo	Sex
Estado civil	Marital status
Fecha de nacimiento	Date of birth
Lugar de nacimiento	Place of birth
Nº de pasaporte	Passport number
Expedido en	Issued in
Fecha	Date
Firma	Signature

DON'T PANIC!

HELP

¡Socorro! ⎫ *¡Auxilio!* ⎭	Help!
¡Emergencia!	Emergency!
¡Paso, paso!	Let me by!
¡Necesito un médico!	I need a doctor!

¿Me puede ayudar, por favor?	Can you help me please?

In an emergency, dial 091 and ask for:

la policía	police
una ambulancia	ambulance
los bomberos	firemen

Spanish police (usually armed):

la Policía Nacional	National police
la Policía Urbana	Local police/traffic wardens
la Policía de Tráfico/ la Guardia Civil	Traffic police

LOST PROPERTY

He perdido el pasaporte	I've lost my passport
He perdido la maleta	I've lost my suitcase
He perdido el bolso	I've lost my handbag

SOMETHING HAS BEEN STOLEN

Me han robado la cartera	My wallet's been stolen
Me han robado el coche	My car's been stolen

LOST FOR WORDS

¿Habla inglés?	Do you speak English?
Lo siento. No hablo español	I'm sorry, I don't speak Spanish

SIGNS

Entrada	Way in
Salida	Way out
Empujad	Push
Tirad	Pull
No está permitida la entrada	No entry

Prohibido fumar	No smoking
Prohibido el paso	No entry/No trespassing
No funciona	Out of order
Lavabos	Toilets
Señoras	Ladies
Caballeros	Men

KEY TO EXERCISES

1 HELLO

GREETINGS AND GOODBYES

1 Hola, buenos días, Tomás. ¿Cómo estás?/¿Qué tal?
2 Adiós, buenas noches.
3 ¿Cómo está (usted) Sra González?
4 Bien, gracias. ¿Y tú?

AT THE CAFETERIA

5 Oiga, camarero.
6 (Quiero) un café con leche.
7 (Quiero) una cerveza.
8 (Quiero) vino blanco y aceitunas.

MIX AND MATCH

9 Buenos días
10 Buenas tardes
11 Agua fría
12 Vino tinto
13 Café solo

FILL IN THE GAPS

14 Hola, buenos *días*. ¿Cómo *está* usted?
    Muy bien, *gracias*. ¿Y *usted*?
15 ¿Qué va a *tomar*?
    Un café.
    ¿Solo *o* con leche?
    Con leche, *por favor*.

16 Soy Pepe. ¿*Y* tú?
Soy Carlos.
17 ¿*Cómo* estás?
Bien, *gracias*. ¿Y tú?
18 ¿*Qué* tal?
Muy bien. ¿Y *usted*?

IN A BAR

19 ¿Qué tienen para beber?
20 ¿Tienen tapas?
21 Cerveza y jamón, por favor.

TRANSLATE INTO SPANISH

22 ¿Qué tal la cerveza?
23 Quiero un café.
24 Vino tinto, por favor.
25 No, gracias.
26 La cerveza está buena.
27 El vino está frío.

2 SHOPPING

AT THE GROCER'S

1 Quiero medio kilo de uvas, un cuarto de kilo de jamón
serrano, dos litros de vino tinto y cuatro kilos de tomates.
2 No, nada más, gracias. ¿Cuánto es?/¿Cuánto es en total?
3 Aquí tiene, mil cuatrocientas veintisiete.

MIX AND MATCH

4f ● 5c ● 6h ● 7e ● 8b ● 9a ● 10d ● 11g

AT THE CHEMIST'S

12 ¿Tiene algo para el dolor de oídos?
13 ¿Tiene algo para las quemaduras de sol?
14 ¿Cuánto es en total?
15 Aquí tiene. Muchas gracias. Adiós.

AT THE SHOE SHOP

16 Quiero unos (un par de) zapatos marrones, número 42.
17 ¡Qué caro! ¿Tiene algo más barato?
18 No me gustan nada. ¿Tiene otro modelo?

AT THE POST OFFICE

19 Quiero cinco sellos para Europa.
20 Quiero enviar una postal.

MIX AND MATCH

21 Una blusa amarilla
22 Unas camisas blancas
23 Unos zapatos negros
24 Un abrigo rojo

FILL IN THE BLANKS

25 SEÑORA   Buenas días. *Quiero* un *traje*.
     EMPLEADA   ¿De *qué* talla?
     SEÑORA   La cuarenta.
     EMPLEADA   ¿Le gusta *éste*?
     SEÑORA   Sí, éste me *gusta* mucho. *¿Qué* precio *tiene*?
     EMPLEADA   Veintitrés mil ochocientas *pesetas*.
     SEÑORA   ¡*Qué* caro! ¿Tiene algo más *barato*?
     EMPLEADA   No, no hay *nada* más barato. Lo *siento*.

3 OUT AND ABOUT

IN THE STREET

1 (Oiga, perdone . . .) ¿dónde está el museo?
2 ¿Dónde hay una farmacia?
3 ¿Hay una parada del autobús por aquí?

I'M A FOREIGNER

4   Lo siento, no hablo español.
5   Soy extranjero/a.

GETTING TO THE PLAZA DE ESPAÑA

6   ¿Cómo puedo ir a la Plaza de España?
7   ¿Sabe qué autobús?
8   Muchas gracias. Adiós.

FILL IN THE GAPS

9   ISABEL   Oiga, *perdone*. ¿Dónde *hay* una farmacia?
   SEÑOR   En *la* calle Mayor.
   ISABEL   ¿Está *lejos*?
   SEÑOR   No, está *muy* cerca. A unos dos *minutos* a pie.
   ISABEL   Muchas *gracias*.
   SEÑOR   *De* nada.

TELL THE TIME

10   Las doce y cuarto
11   Las nueve y media
12   Las tres y diez de la tarde
13   Es casi la una
14   Las siete menos diez
15   La una y veinticinco
16   Son casi las tres menos cuarto
17   A las once de la mañana
18   A la una menos cuarto de la tarde
19   A las once menos cinco de la noche

ASKING DIRECTIONS

20   Sí, muy cerca, Plaza Mayor esquina Garcilaso.
21   (Está) en la calle Cervantes.

22 En la calle Larra, enfrente del estanco.
23 En el número 90 de la calle Mayor.
24 Cervantes esquina Quevedo.
25 En la calle Mayor.

AT THE HOTEL

26 Quiero una habitación doble, con cama de matrimonio y vistas al mar.
27 Para cinco noches.
28 Sí, estas cuatro maletas.
29 ¿Cuánto es por noche?

ASKING FOR A SINGLE ROOM

30 Quiero una habitación individual con baño.
31 Para tres noches.
32 ¿A qué hora sirven el desayuno?

TRANSLATE INTO SPANISH

33 ¿Se puede fumar en la cafetería?
34 ¿Se puede aparcar en esta plaza?
35 ¿Se puede visitar la catedral?
36 ¿Se puede ir en metro?
37 ¿Se puede reservar una habitación?

4 GETTING TO YOUR DESTINATION

RENTING A CAR

1 Buenos días. Quiero alquilar un coche de cuatro puertas.
2 Para un mes.

AT THE TRAVEL AGENT'S

3 Quiero ir a Mallorca.
4 Quiero ir en barco.

5 ¿Cuánto dura el viaje?
6 Quiero un billete de ida.

AT THE RAILWAY STATION

7 ¿Qué trenes hay para Bilbao?
8 ¿Cuánto cuesta?
9 Quiero dos billetes de ida y vuelta.

TRANSLATE INTO SPANISH

10 ¿A qué hora sale el tren?
11 ¿A qué hora llega el avión?
12 ¿Cuánto cuesta ir a Valencia en tren?
13 ¿Cuánto dura el vuelo?
14 ¿Hay un tren para Zaragoza hoy?
15 Quiero alquilar un apartamento para el mes de agosto.
16 ¿Qué precio tiene el Expreso?

FILL IN THE GAPS

17 SEÑOR   Buenos *días*. *Quiero* un billete de *ida* para
                     Londres.

      EMPLEADO   Hola, *buenos* días. ¿Cuándo *quiere* ir?

      SEÑOR   *El* veintinueve *de* julio.

      EMPLEADO   ¿Y *volver*?

      SEÑOR   *Una* semana *después*. El cinco de *agosto*.

      EMPLEADO   Muy *bien*.

      SEÑOR   ¿Cuánto dura el *vuelo*?

      EMPLEADO   Una hora y *tres* cuartos. ¿Cómo *va* a pagar?

      SEÑOR   En *efectivo*. ¿A qué *hora* sale?

      EMPLEADO   A *las* once de *la* mañana.

      SEÑOR   ¿Y a qué *hora* *llega*?

      EMPLEADO   *A* las *once cuarenta y cinco*, hora local.

5 LIVING IN SPAIN

A CONVERSATION

1   ¿Cómo se llama usted?
2   ¿De dónde es usted?
3   ¿Es usted casado o soltero?
4   ¿Qué profesión tiene usted?
5   ¿En qué ciudad vive usted?
6   ¿En qué zona?

IN A RESTAURANT

7   ¡Oiga, camarero!
8   ¿Qué hay de primero?/¿Qué tienen de primero?
9   ¿Qué hay de segundo?/¿Qué tienen de segundo?
10   ¿Qué hay de postre?/¿Qué tienen de postre?
11   Quiero gazpacho, merluza y helado.

THE BILL, PLEASE

12   Camarero, ¿me puede dar la cuenta, por favor?
13   Aquí tiene, mil pesetas. Quédese con la vuelta.

FILL IN THE GAPS

14   CARLOS   *¿Qué* tal el vino?
     FELISA   *Está* muy bueno.
     CARLOS   ¿Le *gusta* la paella?
     FELISA   *Me* gusta muchísimo.
15   MIGUEL   *¿Qué* hay de primero?
     CAMARERO *Hay* consomé o gazpacho.
     MIGUEL   ¿Y de *segundo*?
     CAMARERO Hay merluza *o* pollo.
     MIGUEL   ¿Y *de* postre?
     CAMARERO Hay, flan *fruta* del tiempo o arroz con leche.

CAN YOU GET BY?

WHERE WOULD YOU BUY WHAT?

1d ● **2f** ● **3b** ● **4e** ● **5g** ● **6a** ● **7h** ● **8c**

CHOOSE THE CORRECT ANSWER

9c ● **10g** ● **11b** ● **12i** ● **13d** ● **14j** ● **15e** ● **16a** ● **17h** ● **18f**

WRITE THE FOLLOWING NUMBERS IN SPANISH

19 mil uno
20 ochenta y ocho
21 sesenta y nueve
22 trescientos setenta y cinco
23 siete coma cinco
24 doce mil trescientos sesenta
25 cero coma dos
26 quince por ciento
27 un millón, setecientas cincuenta mil, ochocientas
       veinticinco pesetas
28 mil novecientas noventa y nueve pesetas

TRANSLATE THE FOLLOWING

29 ¿Dónde están los lavabos/servicios?
30 Quiero un par de zapatos.
31 No me gustan los pantalones marrones.
32 Quiero ir a la playa.
33 Hoy es el quince de diciembre.
34 ¿En qué puedo servirle?
35 ¿Cuántos años tienes?
36 ¿Cuánto cuesta el billete de avión?
37 Hablo un poco de español.
38 Soy británico/a, y estoy en España de vacaciones.

FILL IN THE GAPS

39 EMPLEADO   Buenas *tardes*. ¿Cómo *se* llama *usted*?

CLIENTE   *Buenas* tardes. Me *llamo* Peter.

EMPLEADO   ¿Y de *apellidos*?

CLIENTE   Robinson.

EMPLEADO   ¿*Dónde* ha nacido *usted*?

CLIENTE   En Gran Bretaña. Soy *británico*.

EMPLEADO   ¿En qué *ciudad* vive *usted*?

CLIENTE   *Vivo* en Londres.

EMPLEADO   ¿*Está* usted *casado* o *soltero*?

CLIENTE   Casado.

WORD LIST

Words listed in the Reference Section are not included in this word list.

a   at, to
abierto/a   open
el abrigo   coat
abrir   to open
el abuelo/la abuela   grandfather/grandmother
el aceite de oliva   olive oil
la aceituna   olive
adiós   goodbye
el aeropuerto   airport
la agencia de viajes   travel agent's
el agua (f.)   water
el agua (f.) **mineral**   mineral water
ahora   now
el ajo   garlic
alemán/alemana   German

el alemán   German language
al fondo   at the back
algo   something, anything
algunos/as   some
la almeja   clam
almorzar   to have a snack or light lunch
el almuerzo   snack, light lunch
alquilar   to rent
allí   there
a mano derecha   on the right-hand side
a mano izquierda   on the left-hand
el amigo/la amiga   friend
andando   on foot, walking
el año   year
el aparcamiento   car park
aparcar   to park
el apartamento   apartment, flat

aparte separate, separately
el apellido surname
el aperitivo snack
a plazos in instalments
aprender to learn
aproximadamente approximately
aquí here
el arroz rice
australiano/a Australian
el autobús bus
el autocar coach
el automóvil car
la autopista motorway
a ver let's see
el avión plane
ayer yesterday
la azafata air hostess
el azúcar sugar
azul blue

B - *LA LETRA 'BE'*

bajo/a short, low
el banco bank
el bañador swimsuit
el baño bath
el bar bar
barato/a cheap
el barco ship
la barra bar (counter), loaf
el barrio district, quarter
bastante considerably

beber to drink
la bicicleta bicycle
bien well
el billete ticket
blanco/a white
la blusa blouse
el bocadillo large filled roll
el bolso handbag
bonito/a nice, pretty
el bonito tuna fish
el bono bus or tube pass
la bota boot
la botella bottle
británico/a British
bueno/a good
¡Buen viaje! Have a good trip!

C - *LA LETRA 'CE'*

el caballero gentleman
la cabeza head
la cabina de teléfonos phone box
cada each
el café coffee
la cafetería cafeteria, cafe
la caja de cambios gear box
el cajero/la cajera cashier
el calamar squid
el calcetín sock
caliente hot
el calor heat

la calle street
la cama bed
el camarero/la camarera waiter/waitress
cambiar to change
la camisa shirt
el camping campsite
el campo countryside
la carne meat
el carnet de identidad identity card
la carnicería butcher's
caro/a expensive
la carretera road
la carta menu, letter
la casa house, home
casado/a married
casi nearly
el castellano Castilian language
castellano/a Castilian
el castillo castle
la catedral cathedral
el catalán Catalan language
catalán/catalana Catalan
la cebolla onion
la cena supper
cenar to have supper
el centro centre, town centre
cerca near
el cerdo pork, pig

cerrado/a closed
cerrar to close
certificado/a registered
la cerveza beer
el cigarrillo cigarette
la ciudad city, town
claro/a light (colour)
claro of course
el coche car
la cocina cuisine, kitchen
coger to take
la colegiata collegiate, church
el colegio school
el color colour
la coma comma
comer to eat
el comercio business, shop, commerce
la comida lunch, dinner, meal
la comisaría de policía police station
¿Cómo? how? what?
comprender to understand
con with
el coñac cognac, brandy
el conductor/la conductora driver
con gas fizzy
la copa glass
costar to cost
creer to think, to believe
la crema cream

el **cruce** crossroads
¿**Cuál?** Which one?
¿**Cuándo?** When?
¿**Cuánto/a?** How much?
¿**Cuántos/as?** How many?
el **cuarto** quarter
la **cuenta** bill, account

CH – LA LETRA 'CHE'

el **champiñón** mushroom
la **chaqueta** jacket
el **cheque** cheque
el **chorizo** Spanish salami
la **chuleta** chop

D – LA LETRA 'DE'

danés/danesa Danish
dar to give
de of
de la mañana a.m., in the morning
de la noche p.m., at night
de la tarde p.m., in the afternoon
del mediodía (12) noon
de nada not at all
de primera clase first class
de segunda clase second class

de vacaciones on holiday
deber to owe
decir to say
dentro de in, inside, within
la **derecha** right
desayunar to have breakfast
el **desayuno** breakfast
el **descuento** discount
desde from
desear to wish
después later, after, then
el **día** day
diario/a daily
el **diccionario** dictionary
diferente different
la **dirección** address
doble double
la **docena** dozen
el **dolor** pain, ache
¿**Dónde?** Where?
la **ducha** shower
durar to last

E – LA LETRA 'E'

la **edad** age
el/la the
él he
ella she
el **embrague** clutch
empezar to start, begin

el empleado/la
empleada clerk,
employee
en in, at
en efectivo by cash
encantado/a delighted,
it's a pleasure
encantar to delight
enfrente de opposite
la ensalada salad
entonces then
la entrada entrance
entre between
enviar to send
el equipaje luggage,
baggage
escocés/escocesa
Scottish
ese/a that
esos/as those
España (f.) Spain
el español Spanish
language
el español/la
española Spanish
person
español/a Spanish
los espárragos asparagus
las espinacas spinach
el esposo/la
esposa husband/wife
esquiar to ski
la esquina corner
la estación station, season

el estado civil marital
status
los Estados
Unidos United States of
America
el estanco tobacconist's
estar to be
el este east
este/a this
el estómago stomach
estos/as these
estupendo/a super,
wonderful
Europa (f.) Europe
exacto/a exact
el extranjero/la
extranjera foreigner
extranjero/a foreign

F – LA LETRA 'EFE'

fácil easy
la familia family
el farmacéutico/la
farmacéutica chemist
la farmacia chemist's
el faro lighthouse
el final end
firmar to sign
la foto photograph
el francés French language
francés/francesa
French
la fresa strawberry
el frío cold

frío/a cold
frito/a fried
la fruta fruit
la frutería fruit shop
el fuego light, fire
fumador smoking (compartment)
fumar to smoke
la función show

G – *LA LETRA 'GE'*

las gafas de sol sunglasses
galés/galesa Welsh
las gambas prawns
el gallego Galician language
gallego/a Galician
la galleta biscuit
el garaje garage
la gasolina petrol
la gasolinera petrol station
la gira tour
girar to turn
la gota drop
gracias thank you
el gramo gramme
Gran Bretaña (f.) Great Britain
grande big
la guía guide
el guisante pea
gustar to please

H – *LA LETRA 'HACHE'*

la habitación room
hablar to speak
el hambre hunger
hasta until, to, as far as
hay there is/there are
el helado ice-cream
el hermano/la hermana brother/sister
el hijo/la hija son/daughter
los hijos children
hola hello
holandés/holandesa Dutch
el hombre man
el hombre de negocios business man
la hora hour, time
el horario timetable
el hospital hospital
el hotel hotel
hoy today
el huevo egg

I – *LA LETRA 'I'*

ida y vuelta return (ticket)
el idioma language
el impuesto tax
incluido/a included
incluir to include
la indigestión indigestion

individual single (room, compartment)
Inglaterra (f.) England
el inglés English language
el inglés/la inglesa English person
inglés/inglesa English
la insolación sun stroke
interesante interesting
ir to go, to get to
irlandés/irlandesa Irish
la izquierda left

J - *LA LETRA 'JOTA'*

el jamón ham
el jamón de York cooked ham
el jarabe cough mixture
el jerez sherry
justo/a right, exact

K - *LA LETRA 'KA'*

el kilo kilogramme
el kilómetro kilometre

L - *LA LETRA 'ELLE'*

al lado de next to
el lavabo washbasin
los lavabos toilets
la leche milk
la lechuga lettuce

lejos far
la libra pound
libre free, unoccupied
una librería a bookshop
un libro a book
el limón lemon
el litro litre
local local
los/las the (plural)
lo siento I'm sorry
luego later, then

LL - *LA LETRA 'ELLE'*

llamar to call
llamarse to be called
la llave key
llegar to arrive
lleno/a full
llevar to carry, wear, have

M - *LA LETRA 'EME'*

la madre mother
el maestro/la maestra schoolteacher
mal bad, badly
la maleta suitcase
la mantequilla butter
la manzana apple
la mañana morning
mañana tomorrow
la manteca lard
el mapa map

el mapa de carreteras   road map
el mar   sea
el marido   husband
más   more, plus
media noche (f.)   midnight
las medias   stockings
medio/a   half
mejor   better
el melocotón   peach
el melón   melon
menos   less, to
el menú   the menu
el mercado   market
merendar   to have tea
la merienda   tea
la merluza   hake
la mermelada   jam
la mermelada de naranja   marmalade
el mes   month
el metro   underground, tube
mi   my
mirar   to look
mismo/a   same
el modelo   design, style, model
el momento   moment
la montaña   mountain
mucho/a   much, a lot
la mujer   woman, wife
la mujer de negocios   business woman

el museo   museum
muy   very

N - *LA LETRA 'ENE'*

nacer   to be born
la nacionalidad   nationality
nada   nothing
nadar   to swim
la naranja   orange (drink and fruit)
negro/a   black
el niño/la niña   boy/girl
no   no, not
la noche   night
no fumador   non-smoking (compartment)
el nombre   name
el norte   north
norteamericano/a   American, from the US
nosotros/as   we
nuestro   our
el número   number, shoe size

O - *LA LETRA 'O'*

o   or
el oeste   west
la oficina   office
la oficina de Correos   post office

oiga excuse me!
otro/a other, another

el padre father
los padres parents
pagar to pay
el País Vasco the Basque country
el pan bread
la panadería bread shop
los pantalones trousers
el paquete parcel, box, packet
el par pair
para for
la parada (del autobús) bus-stop
el parador state-owned hotel
el pasaje fare for ship or plane
el pasaporte passport
el paseo walk, stroll
el pastel cake
la pastilla tablet, pastille
la patata potato
las patatas fritas chips, crisps
el patio patio
la película film
pensar to think
pequeño/a small

la pera pear
¡Perdone! Sorry! Excuse me!
el periódico newspaper
el permiso de conducir driving licence
permitir to allow
pero but
la pescadería fish shop
el pescado fish
el pie foot (*a pie* on foot)
el pimiento pepper
el plano plan
la planta storey, plant
el plátano banana
el plato plate, dish, course
la playa beach
la plaza square, place, market
un poco a little
poco/a little
poder can, to be able to
el policía policeman
la policía police
la pollería poultry shop
el pollo chicken
por favor please
por noche per night
porque because
¿Por qué? why?
la postal postcard
el postre dessert
el precio price
preferir to prefer
presentar to introduce

primero/a first

el primer plato first course

la profesión profession, job

el profesor/la profesora teacher **prohibido/a** forbidden

la propina tip **próximo/a** next

el pueblo village, small town

el puente bridge

la puerta door, boarding gate **pues** well, of course

Q – LA LETRA 'CU'

¿Qué? What?

las quemaduras de sol sun burn **querer** to want, to love

el queso cheese

¿Quién? Who?

R – LA LETRA 'ERRE'

el/la recepcionista receptionist **recto/a** straight, direct

el Reino Unido United Kingdom **reservar** to reserve

el restaurante restaurant

rojo/a red

la rueda wheel

S – LA LETRA 'ESE'

saber to know **salir** to go out, leave

la sed thirst **segundo/a** second

el segundo plato second course

el sello stamp

la semana week

el señor man, sir, Mr

la señora woman, madam, Mrs

la señorita young lady, Miss

el servicio service

los servicios toilets **servir** to serve **si** if **sí** yes

la siesta nap **siga** follow (from the verb **seguir** – to follow) **sin gas** still, uncarbonated

el sol sun **solo/a** alone **sólo** only, just **soltero/a** single

la sopa soup

la sopa de ajo garlic soup

el sueño sleep, dream

el supermercado supermarket

un supositorio suppository

su   your (polite), his, her
el sur   south

el tabaco   tobacco, cigarettes
la talla   size
el taller   workshop
también   also
tarde   late
la tarde   afternoon
la tarjeta   card, credit card
el taxi   taxi
el té   tea
el teléfono   telephone
el telegrama   telegram
el tendero/la tendera   shopkeeper
tener   to have
la ternera   veal
el ticket   tube ticket
el tiempo   time, weather
la tienda   shop
la tienda de comestibles   grocer's
el tipo   type, sort **todo/a**   all, every
todo   everything
todos   everybody
tomar   to take, to have
tomar el sol   to sunbathe
tomar fotos   to take photographs

el tomate   tomato
la tónica   tonic water
la tortilla   omelette
la tos   cough
el total   total (*en total*   in total) **trabajar**   to work
el trabajo   work, job
el traje   suit
el/la transeúnte   passer-by
la travesía   journey (by ship)
el tren   train **tú**   you (singular, informal)
tu   your

último/a   last **un/una**   a **unos/unas**   some
urgente   urgent, express
usted   you (singular, formal) **ustedes**   you (plural, formal)
la uva   grape

las vacaciones   holiday
¡Vale!   OK! **valer**   to be worth, to cost
¡Vamos!   Let's go!
el vasco   Basque language
vasco/a   Basque
el vaso   glass **vender**   to sell **ver**   to see

la verdulería greengrocer's

las verduras vegetables

el vestido dress

la vía platform

el viaje trip, journey

el viaje de negocios business trip

el vino wine

el vino de la casa house wine

visitar to visit

vivir to live

volver to return

vosotros/as you (plural, informal)

el vuelo flight

la vuelta change, return, turn

vuestro your

W – 'UVE DOBLE'

X – LA LETRA 'EQUIS'

Y – 'I GRIEGA'

y and

ya already, all right

yo I

Z – LA LETRA 'ZETA'

la zanahoria carrot

el zapato shoe

la zona area

el zumo juice

el zumo de tomate tomato juice

N O T E S

NOTES